Secrets of a Serendipitous Millionaire

Madeleine Kay

Secrets of a Serendipitous Millionaire

How to Succeed
at Anything
You Want

Chrysalis Publishing

Copyright © 2015 by Madeleine Kay

All rights reserved. No part of this publication may be reproduced or transmitted in any form or by any means, mechanical or electronic, including photocopying and recording, or by any informational storage and retrieval system, without permission in writing from the Author or Publisher (except by a reviewer, who may quote brief passages and/or show brief video clips in a review).

Disclaimer: The Publisher and the Author make no representations or warranties with respect to the accuracy or completeness of the contents of this work and specifically disclaim all warranties, including without limitation warranties of fitness for a particular purpose. No warranty may be created or extended by sales or promotional materials. The advice and strategies contained herein may not be suitable for every situation. This work is sold with the understanding that the publisher is not engaged in rendering legal, accounting, or other professional services. If professional assistance is required, the services of a competent professional person should be sought. Neither the Publisher nor the Author shall be liable for damages arising herefrom. The fact that an organization or website is referred to in this work as a citation and/or potential source of further information does not mean that the Author or the Publisher endorses the information the organization or website may provide or recommendations it may make. Further, readers should be aware that internet websites listed in this work may have changed or disappeared between when this work was written and when it is read.

ISBN 10: 1477534687
ISBN 13: 978-1477534687

Major portions of this book previously appeared in *Serendipitously Rich*. Reprinted here with permission of the publisher.

Published by:

Chrysalis Publishing
Flat Rock, NC 28731

DEDICATION

*To Everyone Who Has Ever Wished to Be Rich ...
There **is** hope!*

ALSO BY MADELEINE KAY
(Available in both paperback and electronic formats)

Living Serendipitously...keeping the wonder alive

Living with Outrageous Joy

Serendipitously Rich ... How to Get Delightfully, Delectably, Deliciously Rich (or anything else you want) in 7 <u>Ridiculously</u> Easy Steps

The 7 Secrets to Living with Joy and Riches

Savoring Life ... Not Just Working At It
8 Principles for Living a Delicious Life

The 12 Myths about Money

The UMM Factor ... (what you need in order to succeed)

Internet Success for Beginners ... 7 Secrets Revealed

Internet Success for Beginning Entrepreneurs ... 7 Secrets Revealed

Internet Success ... 12 Secrets Revealed

Scats ... scattered thoughts on just about everything

The Serendipity Handbook

Coming soon

How Will I Ever Get Over My Happy Childhood
(Stories)

Contents

. . . .

Note from the Author 13

Introduction 15

Money is Energy 23

Chapter 1
The 12 Myths about Money 27
Creating New Myths to Catapult You into Wealth 39

Chapter 2
Secret #1 – Decide 43
What Interferes with Making a Decision 61
Things You Can Do to Help You Decide 62
Action Tip – Secret #1 63

Chapter 3
Secret #2 – Act 67
Points to Remember 82
Action Tips – Secret #2 83

Chapter 4
Secret #3 – Believe 89
Action Tips – Secret #3 100
The Dare 102

Chapter 5
Secret #4 – Serendipity 105
Qualities of Serendipity 114
Shoulds to Delight In 115
Action Tips – Secret #4 117

Chapter 6
Dare to Be Rich 123
The 4 Secrets to Getting Rich 130
Action Tips for Getting Rich 131

Serendipity Is *132*
The Double Dare *133*

. . . .

About the Author *135*

Other Books by Madeleine Kay *136*

Links and Resources *142*

Notes *144*

Note from the Author

I was astounded to discover how easy it is to become rich…how easy it is to succeed and acquire real wealth with relative ease and to do, be and have everything you want.

So many of us have created such a mystique around the subject of money – such a mystery about "The Rich" – that becoming rich has felt unattainable because it has always seemed to be something reserved for "them" not "us."

Well, I want to tell you that "we" are "them"…

and that becoming one of "them" is simpler than you ever thought, easier than you ever imagined, and more fun than you ever dared dream.

I want to share with you the secrets I have discovered for getting rich – the four ridiculously easy, sure-fire steps for acquiring money, becoming wealthy, and for succeeding at anything…no…everything you want in life.

EnjOy,

INTRODUCTION

Have you ever noticed the words we use when referring to money? "He's filthy rich!" or "She's obscenely wealthy." We refer to money as "dirty" and people who care about or want or have money as greedy and selfish.

No wonder so many people don't have money and live in lack and then wonder why! They don't want money. They don't want to be filthy, obscene, greedy or selfish… so on a very strong subliminal level, probably most of you who do not now have money or are not wealthy, are in your present situation because you don't and haven't ever really wanted money.

I know you probably find that hard to believe and are even sitting there saying, "Of course I want money! Who doesn't?"

You don't. And I didn't either for a long time. Oh sure, you say you want money, you want to get out of debt, you want to succeed. But the part of you that really on a core, elemental level is determining what you really want and therefore, will get, have and experience, has disdain for money, little or no respect for money, and doesn't even like money.

I realized this a while ago when I was having financial difficulties and was in fact, in major debt. Although I said I wanted money, I wanted to be rich, I wanted to get out of debt…on a deep core level, I did NOT want money because I thought it would change who I was. I thought it would diminish me in some way.

THE ISSUE WITH MONEY

Let me back track a little to explain because so many of us have issues with money that are so subtle and totally unknown to our conscious minds that we aren't even aware of them. Our relationship with money is very complex and often confusing. So let me explain a few things and see if any of these apply to you. See if they resonate with you. Be honest with yourself because if you ever want to be rich…really rich…you have to recognize, acknowledge and then discard and replace your old beliefs about money, wealth and success with productive new beliefs, which is really hard to do if you're not even aware of your beliefs to begin with.

It's easy to do however, once you become conscious of your beliefs. Then you just replace those beliefs with new ones. If you are reading this book, then you are ready for a change…like getting rid of old clothes that no longer fit you or you no longer feel good in, and replacing them with new ones that make you feel and look like a million bucks!

Wouldn't it be great to put on something every day that you feel just sensational in? Well, that's how your whole life can and should be – every single day can be like a favorite outfit that you love. Every day can and should be special. And…you can do, be and have everything you want…right now, without sacrificing your soul to get it.

I guess that's the key phrase – "without sacrificing your soul to get it" – whatever "it" is. So many of us have been programmed to believe that to become wealthy or be successful, we need to "sell our soul". That we will be forced to compromise our integrity and values and somehow diminish who we are…put our very authenticity into question.

That's how I felt for most of my life. I was an artist, a writer, and felt therefore, that I should not care about money or success. They were beneath me. In fact, I think that if I had written a book years ago and someone or some company had offered me a $500,000 advance or royalty, I would have actually turned it down. I probably would have stuck up my nose and said quite sincerely, "Oh no, I'm an artist. I don't care about money," and walked away.

Now I know that sounds ridiculous to you ... and to me too now because I am making it so obvious. But years ago, it wasn't so obvious to me. I was stuck in "the starving artist syndrome" – that to be a true artist, a great artist, you had to create for one reason only – the love of the art and creating – and you could not, should not, dare not want, care about or even be willing to accept money (especially a lot of money!) for it, because that would somehow taint your artistic integrity and the value of what you had created.

So yes, years ago, I would have walked away from millions and probably did. As we all have. I sabotaged myself and my success so many times, often without even being aware of it...as I am sure so many of you have too.

I had no idea I was doing it though. I thought I was being noble and good and "true to myself." What hogwash! The truth is I had issues about money that I was not even aware of (more about those later). Perhaps I was also afraid of success – the responsibility, the work, the demands and expectations that come with success. Perhaps I was lazy. Perhaps I was just ignorant about a lot of things and needed to do a lot more living and learning before I was ready to be successful...ready to be rich...ready to make friends with money.

Anyway, one morning it hit me that I didn't really want money. I had no respect for money. I didn't even like money. So why should money come to me, I realized. Why in the world would anything or anyone be attracted to or come to someone who doesn't want it, doesn't respect it and doesn't even like it?

Wow! I was stunned! It was an amazing epiphany for me that changed my life. I had mismanaged money – lots of it! I had squandered money, saying, "Oh, it's only money," (I'm sure you've heard that before!) dismissing it as though money was insignificant and had no value at all.

Now I am not saying that money is all-important either. What I am saying is that money, like so many other things in life, is important and can and should not be dismissed. It should not be sought only because we have to have money to live or survive. It should be sought not as an end in itself, but for its exchange value in terms of time, energy, relationships, goods we can enjoy and the service we can do...for the freedom it affords us to fully develop our potential and to use all our talents, without dissipating any of those because we are living in lack, anxiety, worry or fear, which drain all our resources.

Money does indeed have value – positive value. I had gone to such an extreme in my disdain for money, riches and success, because I thought that my disdain and disinterest in them confirmed the fact that I was a good person, an honest person, a sincere person whose values were lofty and noble. Not only did my lack of interest in money *not* make me any of those things, it made me foolish and put me in debt...and seriously affected the quality of my life on every level.

And here's the interesting thing. When I had that epiphany and finally realized the intrinsic value of money – the freedom it affords one to truly live as one wants, to create, to share, to be generous, to live openly and totally from the heart – I felt ashamed of myself. I felt like somehow I had become or admitted that I am a superficial person with no real values at all.

And when I spoke to my son about this book that I wanted to write, I couldn't bring myself to tell him what I really wanted to write about. I kept beating around the bush so I wouldn't have to admit that I wanted to be rich, that I cared about money, and that I actually wanted to write a book about getting rich. I thought he would be disappointed in me.

I kept trying to make the book sound more like a metaphysical book because I still couldn't reconcile myself to the fact that getting rich is a noble goal and that wealth and success are desirable things to aspire to and be proud of.

But my acceptance of money and wealth as lofty goals to be proud of still wasn't complete. I kept backsliding. Every time I thought about writing this book, (and others on the subjects of wealth, success and becoming rich – subjects about which I am now passionate) I shuddered, thinking that my friends and readers would think I had become shallow, that I had sold out, that I was no longer a person with lofty values.

But like Nietzsche says in the prologue to his book *Thus Spake Zarathustra*, I have become "like the bee that hath gathered too much honey; I need hands outstretched to take it." I am so excited about this realization that has absolutely liberated me, that has opened me up to everything life has to offer...that I can't wait to share it with you. I can't wait to tell you how easy it is to transform your life and become truly rich and prosperous.

So yes, I now know that living a rich and abundant life is both noble and desirable; that you can do more good, help more people, and enjoy your life more if you are wealthy rather than poor; that feeling bad about surpassing your parents is not a way of honoring them, but of dishonoring them; that artistic creation has real value and deserves to be compensated just like any other job or profession; and that I and all of us are truly meant to be rich and to do, be and have it all.

I know that our lives, in order to be vibrant, full of vitality, succulent and ripe with possibilities, are waiting for us to claim them in all their splendor, variety and richness. In claiming my riches, I have reclaimed my life... and I invite you to do the same.

Money is Energy

I have heard that said over and over in the last ten years.

Both physics and metaphysics tell us the same thing – that everything is energy.

I get it. I understand it. Well, I sort of understand it in terms of its exchange value and quotient. But I never really got it until about two years ago.

I was visiting a good friend of mine in Canada. She is staggeringly wealthy and has been ever since she was born.

She has always had an unbelievably high energy level, a stamina that leaves everyone else in the dust, and a quality of vitality that never loses its radiant glow and momentum.

This everyone knows about her and just accepts. Like the perennial EverReady® battery, she seems unstoppable...she just keeps going and going and going with an enthusiasm and a level of performance that never wane.

Well, two years ago, while I was visiting her and trying dismally and unsuccessfully to keep up with her, it hit me! I suddenly knew why and how she is the way she is...Money!

Yes – money! Do you realize how much energy people put into thinking about money, making money, planning for money, worrying about money, scrounging for money, shifting things around to get more money...and the list goes on and on?? It's exhausting!

Now imagine a lifetime of doing that! Do you realize the amount of energy a person uses up in his or her lifetime over money concerns?

Now...imagine a lifetime of NEVER doing that! That's right! Can you imagine the energy reserve my friend has that 99.99% of everyone else does not have?

No wonder she has so much more energy than everyone else! She has never, ever had to use or expend a drop of her energy thinking about money, worrying about it, planning for it, doing things to get it – so the "balance" in her energy bank account is filled to the brim and constantly overflowing with unused energy that everyone else has expended.

So, I finally got it! It was no longer a mere abstraction for me when I would read that "Money is energy." I even realized that the saying "spend your energy," is talking about just that – that both money and energy are the currency of our lives. It has given me a new, healthy respect for, and appreciation of, money (both of which I never had before) as something that actually contributes to my happiness, my evolution as a human being and my overall well-being.

Integrating this reality into my life as a person motivated by humanitarian and aesthetic values has been an exciting and liberating challenge. It has opened up the entire world for me and made all things possible...and yes, even desirable.

. . . .

So . . . Enjoy . . . Prosper
. . . and Dare to Be Rich!

The 12 Myths about Money

*B*efore we jump into the first secret to becoming rich and succeeding at whatever you want, let's quickly dispense with some of the limiting beliefs and erroneous myths so many of us have about money, becoming rich and being wealthy and successful, so we can get them out of the way and move on to the real business of becoming rich and successful.

(I am not even going to capitalize, bold or highlight these myths, or even make them stand-alone sentences or paragraphs, because I do not want them to stand out on the page and in your minds.)

Myth #1

*I*t is noble to be poor or at least not too rich. This is a wide-spread myth that is truly insidious and I believe has caused no end of damage to allowing people to believe that they have a right to be rich.

You do not in any way help or honor those who are living in lack by also living in lack. The only way you can help them is by being a shining example of how well they too can live and by teaching them and/or giving them the tools they need to elevate their own standard of living.

Lowering your standard of living or keeping your standards low so you don't hurt, offend or frustrate those who are living at a low standard, not only doesn't help them; it further cements them in their own rut and gives them a convenient excuse not to rise above it.

Myth #2

*I*f I have a lot of money or more than I need, then I am taking something away from others who could use it more. This myth is based on a belief in a finite supply of resources and riches.

There is however, an infinite supply of resources and riches – enough for every other person in this world. Your having a lot, even to excess, does not in any way diminish the chances or opportunities for anyone else to have whatever he or she wants, nor does it take anything away from anyone else.

In fact, it does just the opposite. Your abundance creates an energy of abundance. And since both physics and metaphysics tell us that everything is energy, your wealth and riches just help multiply the wealth and riches that are available and accessible to everyone else.

Myth #3

I should feel guilty about surpassing or living better than my parents. This is a very subtle myth that most people aren't even aware of, and it doesn't even necessarily come from anything your parents may have done or said. In fact, I find it often is totally self-imposed, for a variety of reasons (which I am not even going to get into here because it is too much of a digression and not really relevant).

Not only does not living better than your parents not honor them, it is a way of dishonoring them and all the sacrifices they have made for you. The best way to honor your parents and your ancestors, to celebrate their lives and show appreciation for their sacrifices, is to live as happily, as well and as richly as you possibly can.

In fact, it is the hope and prayer of every parent that their children will have better, easier lives than they have. That is the very reason your parents made those sacrifices in the first place.

Myth #4

Rich people are not very nice and are very superficial. That attitude is to me, supremely arrogant and prejudicial.

Rich people are just like people who are not rich – some are nice, some are not; some are superficial, some are not. It is not the money that makes the person, it is the person's values and character that make him or her who they are.

I think sometimes confidence is mistaken for arrogance, and people who have money tend to have a lot more confidence than those who don't. It is true that many people who do not have much money are often more deferring than those with money. But do not mistake low self-esteem (which many people who do not have much money experience) for humility and character. And do not judge confidence as arrogance and superficiality.

I find also that many rich people are judged by those with less money because of envy or jealousy. Do not envy anyone. There are enough riches and money for everyone. Their having a lot does not take anything away from you and does not cast any aspersions on you, your abilities or your value or self worth. Only you determine your value and self worth. Only you determine how much of anything, including money, you will have.

Myth #5

*I*f I am rich or care about making a lot of money, I will wind up compromising my values and integrity. This myth is steeped in a strong judgmental attitude and arises from a lack of understanding of how the world really works.

Money is just as nice, good, desirable and intrinsically valuable as work, religion, family, nature, sex. It's all part of life and none of it is "bad." It's all good, especially if everything is kept in balance and perspective, if we don't idolize or obsess about any one thing…if we strive to enjoy it all.

Again, I think there is a lot of envy and jealousy associated with this judgment. Since a lot of people don't have the money they would like to have and feel badly about that, they often – either as a defense mechanism or to redirect their own frustration, anger or disappointment with themselves – transfer these emotions onto the wealthy and label them undesirable in some way...and in that way, make themselves feel better about not being one of "them".

Myth #6

*I*f I care about money, it means that I am materialistic. This is one I wrestled with a lot when I was growing up and well into my adult years, especially when I was in a long-term relationship with a man who was the ultimate consumer.

It seems to me that if you truly use and enjoy the things you buy, then that doesn't make you materialistic. If those things enrich your life, then I don't think that makes you materialistic. I believe that materialism is only when a person feels that he or she must have a lot of things, must accumulate a lot to make him or herself feel worthy or accomplished, without any regard for the pleasure, joy and genuine enrichment one experiences from having and using those things.

I think we slap labels on people (ourselves included) and their actions far too quickly and easily without really taking the time to think about or understand the implications, value and intentions of their actions and behaviors.

Myth #7

Wanting to make a lot of money or be rich is not a very worthwhile goal in life. Why not? I am discovering how much fun and exciting it is to make money. Everybody likes money, wants money, needs it and enjoys it...so why wouldn't it be worthwhile?

I remember about ten years ago, I was at my cousin's daughter's wedding and saw my cousin's ex-husband for the first time in years. I heard that he had recently gotten married after a long period of being single. So when I saw him, I said, "Hi, Carey. Congratulations. I am so glad to hear you are so happy;" to which he replied, "I don't know how happy I am, and besides, I'm not so sure happiness is such a worthwhile goal in life."

Wow! That says it all, doesn't it? He is highly educated and quite the intellectual, but I don't think he knows a whole lot about life and living because he is too proud and attached to his own image of himself to admit even the most elemental things about himself and his life.

Happiness is THE goal in life – it is what everyone wants...every single one of us. It is the reason we do everything in our lives...because we think it will make us happy. So why are so many of us reluctant, even ashamed to admit, perhaps even unaware of the fact, that what we really want in life is just to be happy? Why does that seem too shallow or superficial to admit, accept or believe?

Why are so many of us reluctant and even ashamed to admit that we would like to be rich? Why does that make us feel as though we are shallow or superficial, and somehow, less noble...as if wanting to be rich precludes and excludes our wanting to do or be anything else as well?

Myth #8

You need to work very hard (and perhaps even "sell your soul") to make money and get rich. This idea comes from the fact that years ago, life was harder, and perhaps people did have to work harder to make money. I don't know if that was true years ago or just seemed true from the many images we have of the masses during wars and the Depression, of people who may have been culturally and socially hypnotized and programmed with that ethos.

I do know that it is no longer true. You don't have to work hard to make money; you just have to work smart. They are very different. The old fashioned work ethic was, I believe, taken to such an extreme and inculcated in so many people, that many people feel really guilty if they don't work hard, if things come to them too easily. And that's when they begin to subconsciously sabotage themselves – to create problems, to cause difficulties, so they will have to struggle and feel that they are "working for and really earning" whatever they get.

Myth #9

You need money to make money.

This myth is simply a "cop-out." It is, what I believe, the most convenient and least personally emotionally charged excuse for not beginning, not continuing, not believing...not doing anything.

It is a cop-out because everybody had to start somewhere. Everyone (or their predecessors or ancestors) began with nothing...or less than nothing, at some point.

Money, or lack of money, is not the real obstacle to success or getting rich, or anything else you want because money is not where the real power lies. The real power, as anyone in Hollywood, politics, or any business will tell you, is found in passion. With passion, comes enthusiasm, commitment, and energy...and energy is what makes things happen.

From Donald Trump to Oprah Winfrey, you will find endless examples of how passion is more important than money...and infinitely more powerful.

Myth #10

*I*f I want a lot of money or I want to be rich, then I am being selfish. I am always amazed and amused by how people use and misuse words and by how readily people embrace the "love your neighbor" admonition – which I think needs to be rephrased to "love yourself as much as you love your neighbor."

I think most people are much nicer to, more compassionate toward, more understanding and forgiving of others than they are of themselves. The toughest boss I ever had during my entire career was me. I was relentless with myself and was so much kinder and more generous with others.

We are the most critical of ourselves, we demand the most from ourselves, and whenever we want to do something nice, or good or fun for ourselves, we think we are being selfish. Don't we deserve the same kindness and generosity of spirit from ourselves that we give to others?

And why shouldn't we do things for ourselves? What in the world is wrong with that? It's healthy and it fills us up with a love and joy that spill over into everything we do and onto everyone we meet.

Myth #11

I can't be rich because of my present circumstances, my past history, my lack of education, the debt I am in, my children, and the list goes on and on.

When you read the four secrets in this book and begin to understand how things really work – how we get what we decide to have and what we expect – when you begin to understand that you, not some outside force, circumstance or person, determine your prosperity and the quality of your life; you determine everything you have, do or are, then you will become energized and empowered to create the life and the wealth you want...especially once you realize how simple and easy it really is to do.

Myth #12

I don't deserve to be rich. This simple, yet very pervasive belief is probably at the root of most people's circumstances and their current inability to create wealth and become rich.

You DO deserve to be rich. You deserve to have everything you want in life. It's your birthright. So claim it! And claim it with a feeling of entitlement. By entitlement, I do not mean arrogance, but rather with a readiness and an expectation. Claim it with a grateful and humble heart in the belief that you deserve to be as rich as any other person does and you don't have to earn that privilege.

Even the Constitution states that every person is entitled to "the pursuit of life, liberty and the pursuit of happiness." And if being rich makes you happy, then it is your inalienable right to pursue riches and to become rich.

So, let's get started. But before we do, let's completely obliterate any power those old myths may have by rewriting them as bold declarations that empower and energize you.

Creating New Myths to Catapult You into Wealth

Myth #1

IT IS NOBLE AND GOOD TO BE RICH AND HAVE LOTS OF MONEY.

Myth #2

IF I HAVE A LOT OF MONEY OR MORE THAN I NEED, I SET A GREAT EXAMPLE FOR OTHERS OF WHAT THEY CAN HAVE.

Myth #3

I AM THRILLED TO BE LIVING BETTER THAN MY PARENTS DID. I KNOW IT IS WHAT THEY WANT FOR ME.

Myth #4

RICH PEOPLE, LIKE ALL OTHER PEOPLE, ARE KIND, GENEROUS, FUN ...AND HAVE LOTS OF SOUL AND DEPTH.

Myth #5

IF I AM RICH OR CARE ABOUT MONEY, I CAN ENJOY MY LIFE IN SO MANY WAYS AND ON SO MANY LEVELS AND GET TO LIVE ACCORDING TO MY DEEPEST VALUES.

Myth #6

IF I CARE ABOUT MONEY, I GET TO ENJOY THINGS FOR THE AESTHETIC, EMOTIONAL AND PHYSICAL PLEASURE THEY GIVE ME.

Myth #7

WANTING TO MAKE A LOT OF MONEY AND BE RICH IS A LOFTY, WORTHWHILE GOAL IN LIFE.

Myth #8

> I CAN MAKE LOTS OF MONEY WITH EFFORTLESS EASE AND CAN ALSO MAINTAIN MY INTEGRITY AND VALUES.

Myth #9

> MY POWER COMES FROM MY PASSION AND ENTHUSIASM.

Myth #10

> IF I WANT A LOT OF MONEY AND WANT TO BE RICH, I AM BEING AS GOOD TO MYSELF AS I AM TO OTHER PEOPLE.

Myth #11

> I HAVE THE POWER TO DETERMINE MY DESTINY – THE QUALITY OF MY LIFE AND WHAT I CAN DO, BE AND HAVE.

Myth #12

> I DESERVE TO BE RICH.

"Be bold and mighty forces will come to your aid."

Basil King

Secret #1

Decide

Yes, just decide to be rich! I know that sounds obvious...and therefore perhaps a little crazy to tell you to decide to be rich.

But it's not obvious. Most people do everything but decide to be rich. They wish, they hope, they pray, they plead, they beg, they try (more about that later) all different things to get rich. But they don't make the decision to be rich.

We "humans" complicate everything so much that as we agonize over how to get rich, we wind up ignoring the one simple, very basic thing we all have to do that will unlock the door to becoming rich – and that is to make the decision to be rich.

Not that you 1) *want* to be rich, or that you 2) *wish* you were rich, or that you 3) *would like* to be rich. None of these is a decision. Not only are they *not* decisions – they are 1) hopeful and futuristic, and kind of watered down with little or no passion behind it 2) subjunctive, which implies an unreal situation 3) conditional, which is used when there are all kinds of qualifiers, conditions and parameters attached to a situation.

Most people avoid making a decision about almost everything in their lives and don't even realize they are avoiding it...that they are being vague and non-committal. So many of us are not used to being declarative and decisive. It sounds so easy – just decide. But it isn't. Simple, yes; but not easy because "simple" is rarely easy for people. Our brains like to complicate things and often we look for all kinds of convoluted answers and complex solutions to our questions and problems...and in so doing, we miss the very simple solution that is usually right there in front of us.

I remember two years ago when I was in Ottawa visiting a friend of mine. We were walking along the Rideau River, enjoying the varied and magnificent wildlife when I noticed a beautiful bird with a shiny black coat and vibrant colors on its wings, perched on a stone wall. "That's a Red-winged Blackbird," my friend told me. Then he immediately turned around, looking for something. "Where's the other one?" he added. "They usually travel in pairs."

So, the two of us began looking all over the place for the second one – craning our necks, looking up and down, left and right – but we didn't see it anywhere. "Oh well," he said, "I guess there is only one this time." And we began to walk away.

Just then, I exclaimed, "Look! There it is!" Right there – perched on the stone wall directly in front of us – was the second Red-winged Blackbird we were looking for. It was right there in front of us all the time, but we were too busy looking for it everywhere else.

How often we miss the obvious that is so clear and simple and right in front of us...like just deciding to be rich.

HABITS

Most of us have unwittingly developed the habit of being indecisive, of procrastinating, of debating a subject endlessly in our minds (or with others); we are plagued by a whole host of "shoulds" and "should nots" and are generally so tentative, that we don't even know what it really feels like to make a decision – to commit unwaveringly to something. And therefore, we really don't understand the power that doing so wields.

Even marriage and relationships – how many people go into them with the thought, "Oh well, if it doesn't work out, I can always get divorced."

That attitude is deadly for any relationship or marriage. I was in a sixteen-year relationship and after the second year, I felt that it was never going to work out, so therefore, I was not going to commit to it. As a result, I never felt a strong need or desire to really work things out whenever problems arose.

Well, two years ago I was speaking with two friends of mine – a married couple celebrating their thirtieth anniversary. I knew she was a very volatile person who was difficult to live with and that there had been a lot of turmoil in their marriage. So I asked them, "Aren't you surprised that you made it to this point?"

"No, I'm not," her husband replied categorically, and he proceeded to explain something to me that has forever changed my entire perspective on commitment and the power of making a decision.

"During the first few years of our marriage," he said, "we argued constantly, and every time, Lisa would say, 'It looks like we're just going to have to get divorced.' This went on for a few years and the arguments got worse, until I made a decision. I decided that divorce was not an option for us. I decided that we were going to make this work. And I said to Lisa, 'Please don't ever mention divorce again. That is not an option. We are going to make this work!'"

"After that, everything changed for us. We began to look for solutions, rather than focusing on our problems. We began to work as and see ourselves as a team, rather than adversaries. It was difficult, but we had made a decision and we were committed."

Wow! I – who have been commitment-phobic most of my life, thinking that commitment meant limitation, resignation, the "end" – suddenly realized that quite the contrary...making a decision and being committed liberate you.

It takes so much energy to be indecisive, to straddle the fence, to walk in "Limbo". And I even, for the first time, began to wonder if rather than my not making the decision to make my sixteen-year relationship work because I knew it wouldn't...perhaps, just perhaps the converse was true – that it didn't work because I never made the decision to make it work.

So, getting back to deciding to be rich – The very first thing you must do in your quest to be rich is to DECIDE TO BE RICH! It's that simple! Once you do this, everything...and I mean...everything changes.

Your decision repositions you, and your brain and your psyche start to look for ways for you to become rich... or to do, be or have whatever it is you have decided to.

They look for and create ways for you to make money and generate income, rather than wondering if you can. Your decision gets you looking forward, instead of backward. It moves you into the energy of possibility – an energy filled with anticipation and expectation rather than fear, worry and doubt.

Making a decision removes doubt, hesitation, and all those stops and starts that hinder us and stop our forward momentum toward what we desire – the should I, could I, what if, why me, well maybe, I'll give it a try, how will I ever, and on and on ad nauseum with all those staccato melodies we play over and over in our minds. None of this exists any longer once you make a decision. Instead, your energy and focus are now forward-looking rather than on second-guessing yourself.

Once you decide to do, be or have something, an amazing thing happens. Your entire focus, perspective and standpoint shift – you are no longer hoping, wishing, fantasizing, dreaming, praying. Instead, you know, feel certain, see it, feel it, breathe it. It becomes real for you and you begin to live it...and therefore, make it happen.

I have found this with everything in my life – once I decide to do something, I just do it. The difficult part, the important thing, is deciding. But once you decide to do something, you *can* and *will* do it. You *will* find a way.

Perhaps that's why so many people hesitate to make decisions and find all sorts of excuses not to make a decision, because they know...on some subliminal level... the enormous responsibilities that come with making that decision. They know that those responsibilities will require them to stop being lazy, to move outside of their comfort zone, to change their habits and their lifestyle, and to welcome the new and the unknown...all of which is really scary.

They also find it scary to actually – for real – believe that they are about to get what they want. Believe it or not, many people say they want to be rich or famous or loved or successful or happy or whatever, but deep down, they actually find the imminent possibility of getting what they want frightening, overwhelming, and intimidating. And they know (maybe not consciously) that when they make a firm, unwavering decision, they will set themselves in motion and begin to create a momentum that moves them inexorably toward whatever it is they have decided to do, be or have...and that is scary.

Scary for so many reasons – people don't feel worthy, they are afraid they won't be able to handle it, they are afraid their lives will change, that they will lose their friends, that more will be required of them than they are willing or able to do...so they would rather stick with the old, the familiar, the "known", even though it is not what they want. At least they know that life, they know what they have and don't have and they are comfortable with what they know and do not find it so scary.

So ultimately, it is often fear...yes, fear of success that sometimes keeps people from deciding to be rich... or anything else they really want. It is fear that keeps them where they are. Fear and laziness – the refusal, the unwillingness, the hesitation to change their habits, their patterns, their life.

STEPPING INTO WHAT IS POSSIBLE

Making a decision, about anything, puts you in a state of readiness, preparedness and receptivity so you are ready, willing and able to respond to all the things, people and opportunities that can help you achieve what you want.

Making a decision catapults you into the realm of possibilities where all things are possible. When you make a decision, you literally open the door and your mind, so you are aware, receptive, flexible and responsive.

Hopefulness and wishful thinking are replaced by determination and focus on where you are going, rather than on where you are and where you have been. You step into a kind of certainty and a knowing, instead of a tentativeness. You start a process and create a momentum that propel you forward towards whatever it is you want.

WHERE ARE YOU GOING

I am reminded of the story of Christopher Columbus passionately recounted in Andy Andrews' book *The Traveler's Gift*. The main character who, through some time warp, lands aboard Columbus' ship, asks him, "Do you really not know where you are?" to which Columbus replies, (and I paraphrase) *No, but what does that matter? My whole life people have asked me that question about my station in life or what I am doing or what I think I can do. It matters not to me if I know where I am. What does matter is where I am going. Ask me that question. Ask me...Ask me where I am going!*

So, the main character asks Columbus, "Do you know where you are going?" to which Columbus thunderously replies, "Yes! Yes, I do know where I am going. I am going to the New World," which he proceeds to describe in vivid detail, even though he is not physically there yet and has never seen it. He tells the main character that tomorrow morning when the sun rises, land – the New World – will be right there in front of them, just where and as he has imagined it.

Einstein, perhaps the greatest physicist in the world, said, "Imagination is more important than knowledge." Imagination allows you to create a new reality rather than being mired in what is.

WHEN, NOT IF

So, once you make a firm, unwavering decision to be rich – the "if" literally slips out of the equation and it only becomes a matter of "when."

But you must make your decision to be rich with no ambiguity, no reservations, no guilt, no shame, no feelings of unworthiness or fears about not being "noble" enough. No thoughts about "how" to accomplish it, "if" you can accomplish it. No thoughts about "why me?" but rather, "Why not me!?"

Once you make your decision, you are catapulted into a whole new perspective that is now mobilizing and looking for solutions and ways in which you can make money, meet people, and create and respond to opportunities in your life to help you reach your goal.

You literally step out of the hypothetical world of "if" into the very real world of "when", usually without even thinking of "how" you will accomplish what you want. In fact, it is better if you don't work or think too hard because then you can become myopic, linear, anal and develop tunnel vision, like a horse with blinders on.

The whole beauty and wonder of this process of deciding to be rich (or successful or happy or anything, for that matter) is that it mobilizes your resources to help you achieve your goal – so you must be open, flexible, receptive and above all, be willing to think associatively...to see and make associations and connections between seemingly unrelated things so you can recognize and respond to opportunities when they arise.

For example, I remember when I had an advertising agency in Miami and one of my clients was a small resort condominium in Key West. At that time, a resort condominium was a brand new concept and we were not sure what would be the best way to advertise it with my client's limited budget.

During the time we were putting the ad campaign together, I read an interview in *Adweek* magazine with the Marketing Director of Coca Cola. In the interview, he spoke about the strategy they had used when they introduced Diet Coke. He said that at that time, diet soda was new and therefore, not widely popular or accepted. So any ad campaign they ran would first have to convince people to drink diet soda...and then, get them to drink Diet Coke. Rather than doing that, they decided to let their competition spend big money to first convince consumers to drink diet soda. Once that was accomplished, then Coca Cola stepped in with a big ad campaign for Diet Coke.

Voilà, we had our answer. We did not spend my client's limited advertising budget promoting them as a resort condominium, (most people didn't even know what a resort condominium was then). Instead, we promoted it simply as a resort. Then once we got tourists and vacationers to visit or stay at the property, they were made aware of the condominium option.

Associative thinking is definitely an asset once you make a decision to do something because thinking associatively multiplies your options and opportunities exponentially.

Making up your mind to do something is like the organizing principle that allows everything to happen and fall into place, like a kaleidoscope organizes the myriad pieces inside into all different patterns.

Without making a decision however, nothing can happen, unless literally, as a result of blind luck – which does occur occasionally.

But if you want something...anything – to be successful, to have money, to find your soul mate, to be a better parent, to do work that you love, to be happy... anything – all you have to do is decide to do, be or have it and you will because your decision lays the foundation and creates a place for it in your life.

Like in the film *Field of Dreams*. Although the movie is a fantasy, it illustrates an essential principle – if you create a space for something, decide to have it, and then expect it, wait for it, prepare for it...it *will* come, without fail. Maybe not always in the form you expect or think it will, for our thinking is often so limited and often too small and narrow, but it will surely come to fill up the space you have created for it.

All you have to do is decide...Decide to be rich... Decide to be happy...Decide to be healthy...Decide to succeed. Just Decide. Whatever it is you want, decide to be it, have it, do it...and you will.

WHY DOES THIS WORK?

Why? Because, as Einstein tells us, we live in a

friendly universe. Why is the universe friendly? Because it is. Years ago, I was with my cousin's daughter and her four-year old son who kept doing something his mother repeatedly kept telling him not to do. Finally, he looked up at her and simply asked, "Why?" And she replied, without any hesitation, "Because I'm the mommy." I thought that was a great answer!

So why is the universe a friendly place? Because it is benevolent and conducive to the growth and blossoming of all kinds of plants and wildlife; the procreation and survival of a plethora of animals; the creation of incredible natural wonders like the Grand Canyon, trees, the sky and autumn; and miraculous wonders like the flight of the Bumble Bee, people being able to fly, and a Hummingbird being able to stop in mid-air. So why shouldn't it be friendly to us?

Why is the universe a friendly place? Because why have something, an entire world, and not have it be friendly? It just doesn't make sense.

Why is the universe a friendly place? Because it functions according to natural laws, like gravity and centrifugal force, so it is not chaotic or random.

Why? Because the great thinkers of all ages – from Plato to Einstein – have told us that in one way or another, everything in the world, including us, is merely a field of energy and information. And we have the free will to choose how to organize and use that energy and information. It is not predetermined. We choose who we want to be and how we want to live. And we do this by the choices we make. We decide what we get, have, do and experience in life.

And since the world is a mirror, what we put out there is what we get back. What we put into the world is reflected back at us in our experience. And in that way, it really is true that we get what we give. This is not some abstract theory, but an observable fact and natural law.

Perhaps you have heard the expression "Like attracts like." Well, it's true. Have you ever noticed that when you are angry, disgruntled or dissatisfied, everything seems to go wrong and you seem to be surrounded by people with problems and complaints?

And when you are happy, generous and feeling abundant and full of love, you find yourself in "the zone," with everything going right, things just falling into place and in the company of happy, loving, contented people?

So deciding to be rich, happy or successful, will somehow bring rich, happy and successful people, situations and experiences to you. All you have to do is be ready...and respond.

DO ... NOT TRY

In *The Empire Strikes Back*, the second film in the *Star Wars* saga, George Lucas has the wise sage Yoda give the young Luke Skywalker some advice. He tells Luke to:

"Try not...Do or do not...There is no try."

This advice is absolutely invaluable. "Try" is a word that I believe should be banished from the English language. It has been the excuse, the crutch, the "out" for so many people for so many things in their lives.

Once you say "I'll try," you are doomed to fail. Trying is half-hearted. Trying implies that if it doesn't work out or you don't succeed, at least you tried.

Not good enough! Not for something you really want or care about.

Trying is only productive when it is used to experiment or experience something new...but never, never to be used to refer to something you really, deeply, truly desire.

Why doesn't trying work? Because it has no energy to it. Trying, by definition, lacks real passion and commitment – the two things that are absolutely necessary to create momentum.

Momentum is ignited by a decision. By deciding, you activate your "on" switch, your "go" button, your "yes" button that says...*yes* I can, *yes* I will, *yes* I am ready. And that readiness fosters a sense of entitlement. Entitlement, not as arrogance, but as a readiness and a willingness to get what you want...and to expect it.

I remember when I was working as a Media Director at a small advertising agency in Miami. It was my first job in advertising after being an instructor at the university, and I knew nothing about advertising, so my boss hired me at an appallingly low salary (especially for a single mother with responsibilities).

As I learned the industry and got better at my job, which I did very quickly, I would go into my boss's office and ask for a raise, and I always got it – about four or five times in the two and a half years I worked there.

The interesting thing is that as I look back, I realize that I never really went in to "ask" for a raise. It was more like, "OK, I'm ready now. You can give me a raise."

Interesting, isn't it? That's the same psychology and perspective you need to come from when you decide to be rich – that you are not asking at all, but rather, announcing that you are ready to be rich, you are willing to be rich, that you have made up your mind to be rich.

THE UNIVERSAL CATALOG

As I said, I got every raise I "asked" for.

An interesting aside about that...and a story I've repeatedly told my son...is that the receptionist/bookkeeper, who was very good at her job and actually friends with our boss, never received a raise.

Finally one day, exasperated, she went into the owner of the agency and confronted him. "Why is Madeleine always getting raises and I'm not?" He paused a moment, reflected and said, "Because she asks me."

It's as simple as that! It's amazing how often we

overlook the obvious. You have to ask for what you want and you have to be ready for it – willing and able to receive it whole-heartedly, unabashedly and categorically. You have to feel like you deserve it.

We all get what we ask for – literally, almost like ordering out of a catalog. Except in a catalog, things are displayed right there for us, so we know what we are ordering.

In our lives however, most of us either don't really realize what we are asking for; or we don't really directly ask for anything in particular, not clearly and distinctly and passionately and unwaveringly; or we keep changing our minds and then wonder why we don't get what we want; or we are ambiguous and ambivalent.

Most people don't even really know what they want. They know what they don't want, but not what they do want. But knowing what you don't want will not get you what you do want because knowing what you don't want has you looking in the wrong direction – backwards instead of forward. It has you saying "no" instead of "yes." It has you in a state of dissatisfaction rather than anticipation.

PUSH AND PULL

Anais Nin, an extraordinary diarist who was good friends with Henry Miller in 1920's Paris, wrote in her

Third (and I believe, her best) Diary:

"And the day came when the risk to remain tight in a bud was more painful than the risk it took to blossom."

It is the "pull" that attracts us, that calls to us, that ignites our passion and liberates an endless store of energy inside us.

The "push" only causes resistance, sluggishness and drains our energy.

What pulls us toward it, motivates us and gives us energy. A decision made to move toward something is always more productive and energizing than a decision made to move away from something.

Know this: once you make up your mind, about anything, there is no stopping you. Why? Because you strip yourself and the situation down to the bare essentials... you distill everything down to the very core of what works, what you need to do to get whatever you want.

Once you make up your mind and make a decision, you eliminate the extraneous and the hypothetical, so that the reality of what you desire becomes a *fait accompli*. Then it is only a matter of time until the external reality you are experiencing will catch up with and mirror your inner reality.

WHAT INTERFERES WITH MAKING A DECISION

- Laziness
- Ignorance (don't even realize you haven't made or need to make a decision)
- Habit
- Reluctance to move out of your comfort zone
- Fear
- Avoidance of responsibility that comes with getting, being, doing, having what you desire.

. . . .

Fear has energy. Don't resist your fear.
Use that energy and transmute it.

Change the fear and avoidance of the new and the unknown to excitement.

Realize that boredom is draining,
risk is energizing.

Choose to step into what energizes you,
excites you and vitalizes you.

Embrace the new and the unknown
as extraordinary presents, just waiting
for you to unwrap them.

THINGS YOU CAN DO TO HELP YOU DECIDE

- Replace the word "if" with "when."

- Do . . . don't try.

- Forget about what you don't want. Concentrate only on what you DO want. (There is a Swiss custom of filling up and tossing a big bowl of water out of every door in your house for the New Year. This gets rid of all the old things you do not want and ushers in a clean, fresh New Year. You might want to try this. It's simple and anyone can do it.)

- Since "nature abhors a vacuum," once you get rid of what you don't want, you need to fill the space with what you do want. You can write it down, or just think about, dream, declare, or do some activities that exemplify the "you" and the life you do want.

- Begin *savoring* your life … not just working at it. Begin *savoring* getting rich … not just struggling to. Begin *savoring* being successful, not just fantasizing about it. Begin the process of becoming *deliciously* rich … not just filthy or obscenely rich.

ACTION TIP - SECRET #1

There is only one thing you need to do . . .

DECIDE to be rich . . . or whatever else you want

Do whatever it takes, whatever you have to do to get clear, focused and determined. Decide what you want and decide to be it, have it, do it or get it. Make up your mind and then expect it, welcome it, prepare for it, get excited about it...and know it is on its way.

Claude Bristol, author of a wonderful little book titled *The Magic of Believing*, tells the story of when he landed in France in 1918 as a "casual soldier," unattached to a regular company.

Although his basic needs were taken care of by the Army, he found himself with no money to buy things that he wanted, like gum or candy or cigarettes. So, whenever he saw someone lighting up a cigarette or chewing gum, he became acutely aware of and upset about the fact that he had no money to spend on those simple pleasures for himself.

This awareness disturbed him so much, that one night, when he was on a crowded troop train and unable to sleep, he made the decision that he would never be without money again. He decided that when he returned to civilian life, he would have money...lots of it! And with that decision, he says, "The whole pattern of my life was altered at that moment."

. . . .

If there is something you want in your life that you do not now have – whether it's money, a mate, a job you love, fame, success, children, happiness, good health – whatever it is...make up your mind now to have it and forever alter your life in this moment.

*"What you can do, or dream you can, do it;
Boldness has genius, power and magic in it."*

Johann Wolfgang von Goethe

Secret #2

ACT

Do something...Anything. Just get started... even with the seemingly smallest thing.

Don't wait until all conditions are perfect or everything is in place. They will never be. If you wait until they are, the time will never be right and you will never begin because there will always be some new thing, something else...a small little detail that is not the way you want it to be.

So just jump in and do it…do it now.

Mark Burnett, the executive producer of such hit shows as *Survivor* and *The Apprentice* practically "invented" reality TV and revolutionized television in general.

How did he do it? How did this British immigrant who came to this country with very little money and absolutely no knowledge of the entertainment industry and no connections to or with anyone create his own entertainment empire in a relatively short time?

By jumping in with both feet, seizing the moment, taking risks and daring to think big in his pursuit of success.

When Burnett first came to the States, this former British army paratrooper was on his way to South America, but decided to stay in California instead. Finding himself with practically no money and knowing no one, he took a job as a nanny (Yes – a nanny!) to a big Hollywood mogul and his family.

He worked as a nanny for two years, during which time he saw how he wanted to live and became firm in his resolve to someday live that life. In fact, he decided to even live on that same street someday.

When he quit being a nanny, he began to sell t-shirts on Venice Beach and saved enough money from both his endeavors to buy a small piece of real estate, which he then sold, made some money…and began to build his empire and live his dream. (By the way, he did eventually – within just a few years – not only live on that same street, but in the very same house, which he bought from his former boss.)

So not only is it imperative to act – to do something, (the action you take can be small, seem trivial, appear totally unrelated to whatever it is you want – like being a nanny or selling t-shirts is to becoming a producer), but nothing, not even the seemingly most bizarre action, can ever be ruled out as unimportant.

In meteorology, there is a theory called "The Butterfly Effect," which states that a butterfly flapping its wings off the coast of Africa can cause a hurricane in the Atlantic.

So, since everything and everyone is connected in this web of life, if you just begin, if you act and keep on "acting" and "doing," eventually you will wind up where you want to be...often even surpassing your original vision.

PUTTING ON YOUR DIRECTIONAL

I once heard a quote that said, "If you continue heading in the direction you are going, that is where you will end up." It sounds obvious when it's verbalized, but in our actions, it isn't so obvious. Sometimes we continue doing the same thing over and over expecting different results; we continue heading in a certain direction even though we want to go in an entirely different direction.

For example, so many people say they want to be rich, they want to live a certain lifestyle, etc. yet every day, they continue to only associate with the same people they always have who are in the same rut they are in, participate in activities toward which these same people gravitate and shop at and frequent the same places they always have, with the same people they always have.

If you want to rise to a new level – whether it is financial, intellectual, social, or cultural – you must expose yourself to and begin to associate and mingle with people who have already reached that level. You need to go to, frequent or shop at those places that attract those people and embody that lifestyle and level to which you aspire. It's a way of tricking your psyche and your body into believing and beginning to act like those people you desire to live like.

So, making a decision to do something points you in the right direction and turns on your ignition...and acting, or doing something, actually puts you in gear. The rest is all process.

If you can and will make a firm, unwavering commitment to be rich, (or to do, be, or have whatever it is you want) and then act on that decision, you begin to set in motion a process that will eventually lead you to what you desire.

CARPE DIEM

Acting – doing something – is simple, so don't complicate it. Don't get stuck in your mind with deliberations about "should I," "can I," "is it appropriate," "will it lead me to my desired goal." None of those questions matters. And in fact, if you begin deliberating, they will probably hamper you in your pursuit of success.

Why? For so many reasons.

Action that is taken in the moment, while the spark of passion and enthusiasm is lit, is fueled with a momentum and a propulsion that action that is filtered through the often agonizing, laborious and paralyzing deliberation process is not. Once your mind and mental filters enter the process, so does the critic, the censor, the editor, the judge...and they open the door to fear, doubt, procrastination and hesitation.

Now I am not suggesting that anyone act frivolously, foolishly or irresponsibly. In fact, getting back to the original definition of responsible – which means "able to respond" (not react...but respond. There is a huge difference) – I believe that our physiology (our mind/body) has a built-in mechanism that knows when we are ready for something, when we are able to do what it is we want, when we are able to respond organically from within rather than react to something that is without or outside of us. And that mechanism inside us is what helps light that spark. That spark is simply the spontaneous combustion caused by the meeting of readiness and opportunity.

And if we start thinking too much, that spark diminishes...that electrical current gets short circuited... and the moment is lost. And then we must wait for another moment...prepare to ignite another spark. But if we keep "short circuiting" those sparks – those moments – eventually they will come less and less frequently, until eventually, they become like buried cable wires that we have to dig deep to get to, which then takes a huge amount of effort.

A friend of mine, who has always been obsessed with money and fearful of all change, the unknown and any new experience – especially those involving money – was no longer happy, since she retired, living in the same house or neighborhood she had been living in and really wanted to change her life.

An opportunity arose for her to sell her house at a huge profit and move, but she was terrified of moving, of making any change or decision. She didn't sleep nights; spent every waking hour worrying, afraid and depressed; spent hours crying on the phone as I kept urging her to "just do it". To just list the house with a realtor, assuring her that once she did that, once she made the decision and acted on it…*everything* would change. I assured her that the mere fact of her taking some action would rearrange her life, her energy, her perspective and her priorities completely and catapult her into the forward-moving energy of anticipation, excitement and things to do, rather than her present energy of fear and paralysis that were focusing on the security she thought she was losing.

Well, she listened to me, and the instant…literally, the instant she listed the house with a realtor, everything changed. Not only did she become involved in all the details necessitated by her action in preparing the house for sale, looking for a new house, packing, etc., she had finally broken through her lifelong paralyzing fear and totally, totally transformed her life from that day forward.

The energy it took for her to be so afraid was finally released and she became a risk-taker who now has investment properties, tries new things, and is generally quite free-spirited and unafraid – a totally different person who is happier, freer, and much richer.

BODY LANGUAGE

When you act on your decision to be rich (or anything else), readiness is essential. Not readiness as in everything being in place, but readiness in terms of your being congruent within yourself – in what you want; what you have decided to have and are really ready to have or achieve; and what you believe you can, will and deserve to have.

So readiness is really a threshold upon which you stand and a portal through which you are ready to walk in order to claim what it is you desire.

An integral part of readiness means getting to know and trust your intuition because when something is right, you will feel it or sense it in your gut. It will just feel right…and you will know it's right because your gut feeling never lies.

But this feeling is subtle and requires that you begin

to tune into it and to trust it. Begin to notice those feelings in the pit of your stomach, or in your throat, or that hunch you have that just won't leave you alone. Everybody has these hunches, these gut feelings, so just learn to listen to them…and to trust them.

Every successful business entrepreneur and all great thinkers, from Donald Trump to Albert Einstein have more often relied on their intuition, or what they call their "gut" feelings, than on deliberative reasoning. In fact, Trump, in his book, *The Art of the Deal*, talks about making decisions quickly, intuitively and acting on them immediately.

ACT AND WORK SMARTER, NOT HARDER

Throughout many financial and business circles, there is a widely known and accepted theory called the 80/20 Theory. Quite simply, this theory states that 80% of our time and energy are spent on things that only generate 20% of our income, while most of us spend only 20% of our time and energy on those things that generate and are responsible for 80% of our income.

The old work ethic of working hard is not necessarily the most effective way to get what you want. Working smarter is infinitely more effective and a lot more satisfying than working hard.

Which brings me back to energy – the energy with which you act. When you act immediately and quickly, your action is infused with passion, gusto, vitality and a kind of laser-like quality and focus...with an energy that has the ability to mobilize resources, propel you forward, create momentum, and radiate a magnetic energy out into the world around you to touch, communicate and connect you with everything you need to fulfill your desires.

It is the passion, enthusiasm and excitement with which you act that makes you unstoppable...that enables you to get more done in a short period of time, and to do it better, more effectively, efficiently, and with effortless ease...and...to even have fun while doing it.

Let me interject here that the word "act" is not used in a singular sense. It is used as a collective, cumulative, continuous term. For it is essential that you continue to act – to do things, instead of just thinking about them or planning for them.

In most cases, I have found that planning is often an excuse for not beginning, for not doing...and planning often drags out endlessly until it smothers, dampens and dulls any excitement, enthusiasm and passion one might have had, making the thing you wanted to do a monumental task because you have sucked all the life, energy and momentum out of it and you yourself have been reduced to a stand-still – stuck in the quicksand of inertia.

Most people don't realize however, that the word "inertia" has a double meaning – "An object in motion will stay in motion and an object at rest will remain at rest until an opposite action is applied to change that."

Most people usually only focus on the latter and think "inertia" means being stuck, not moving, unable to get started.

But the positive flip side of inertia is that once you have started to move and are in motion, if you remain in motion, then progress and movement will remain relatively easy. But once you stop, then you enter the negative side of inertia and will stay at rest and immobile until something gets you moving again…and it will take much more effort for you to start over from a stand-still position than it would have taken for you to just continue moving once you were already in motion.

That's why implementing those first two secrets is so important. Once you decide what you want and act on that decision, you have mobilized the positive force of inertia – you have set things and yourself in motion. Then all you need to do is stay in motion…and this is usually accomplished with relatively little effort.

Claude Bristol writes that "…persistence gives confidence and continued right mental attitude followed by consistent action will bring success." Persistence does build confidence. Every time you do something, you feel empowered…no matter how small that action is. So the benefits of each action become cumulative and feed the next one.

And consistent action does not mean sequential action at all. It means continuous action. Every day, do something. Just keep moving forward…keep doing things that feel right. Sometimes these things will seem to make no sense at all (as I am sure being a nanny did not to Mark Burnett at the outset). But eventually, a pattern will emerge. Just be willing to be open, diversified and flexible because life is lived and experienced associatively not linearly...so our plans, hopes and dreams are fed by many different and divergent tributaries, and we never know from which source something wonderful and serendipitous will emerge.

So rather than your actions being linear or sequential, it is far more important that they be self-contained – in the moment. Rather than acting based on seeing each act as the next step in the direction of or toward your desired goal, it is more important to be fully present in each action, to be committed to and focused on and in each action so there are no distractions and none of your energy is dissipated...and the benefits are therefore, multiplied exponentially.

So "act" does not mean to go into full implementation immediately. It doesn't mean to start planning. It means to begin taking action – to ask questions...to begin the treasure hunt with an open and expectant heart...to begin connecting the dots with a patience and a knowing that the full picture will emerge.

THE DOMINO EFFECT

Things really started to happen for me only once I

decided to be rich and actually did something about it. I began to do things differently than I did before. I began to do things where previously, I hadn't done anything.

Suddenly, I began meeting people who were staggeringly wealthy and influential, who invited and welcomed me into their circle, and I began to enjoy not only a glimpse into, but also a taste of what that life I wanted for myself was like.

I was invited to speak at a major fund raiser for a children's non-profit that a reader of mine started after reading my book, *Living Serendipitously*. There I mingled with the powerful and upper echelon members of society and politics and luxuriated in five-star Old World hotel accommodations, amenities and treatment that is usually reserved only for VIP's.

Seemingly out of nowhere, suddenly business and creative opportunities, that had been available to me all along, began opening up and materializing and coming to fruition quickly, easily and with almost no effort at all. I began doing things I never had before – writing e-books, offering e-courses and teleseminars, speaking and consulting more.

I began doing a lot more mentoring and coaching in the entire spectrum of all of my areas of expertise, instead of the more limited areas I had been focusing on. I began coaching and mentoring programs to reach and help more people, while building a private, very lucrative and extremely satisfying private coaching and mentoring practice with select clients.

I developed and expanded my company and interests, which I had wanted to do for awhile, into areas I had only dreamed of before – *The Living Serendipitously Institute* and *Living Serendipitously Enterprises* – offering products and services I love and developing new ones I had been wanting to; partnering with other experts and people I'd admired in joint ventures and projects.

Even something as remote as getting my dog into commercials and movies happened. While I was away in Chicago, a casting agent had seen my neighbor walking my dog and went "crazy over him" and said he wanted to cast him in film and on TV...and voilà, a star was born... and an exciting new venture for me that's been both fun and profitable.

It's all been so serendipitous – so absolutely plentiful and abundant – literally like a cornucopia of offerings, opportunities, chance meetings and synchronistic events ever since I *decided*, really *decided* to be rich...and began to *do* something about it.

Once I began acting and doing things, it was literally like opening some magical door out of which spilled more and more. It was almost as though I had turned on some switch and released a storehouse of riches there for the offering, just waiting for me to claim them.

And this prosperity – this abundance – is available to everyone who is ready and willing to just *do* something... anything...to initiate the flow.

ACT OUT OF A DESIRE FOR MORE

I recently became acquainted with a woman who came to me for some writing coaching and mentoring. She told me how happily married she was for thirty years, and then her husband died. For two years, she stayed home alone and was achingly lonely, until one day, she decided she wanted more out of life.

At the same time, a gentleman in a completely different part of the country who had lost his wife two years earlier was also withering away and wallowing in depression and loneliness, until he decided that he had a choice. He could live or he could die, and he decided to live. So he began going to the gym, got himself in shape, and when he felt healthier, better and was ready, he booked a cruise to some exotic destination in Africa…the same cruise this woman had booked passage on.

Well, just like out of one of those cinematic sweeping sagas, they met, fell in love, married, and shared an exotic, exciting life for seventeen glorious years and the kind of romantic love you only read about. And all because each of them decided to do something…to take some action on their decision to get more out of life.

So acting, making one small or large gesture, can change everything. The important thing is to act – to *do* something – which sets in motion a chain of events that take on a life of their own…and you never know where they will lead you.

So when you do act, always operate and act out of desire, not need. Need focuses on lack, the thing you don't have, what you don't want. Desire focuses on what you *do* want and attracts it to you…and will therefore guide you to the right decision. Then just believe…and wait for and expect it to happen.

POINTS TO REMEMBER

Do something…anything. Even if it turns out to be not the best action to have taken, at least you did something. You began...and that is empowering and initiates a momentum.

Do it now. Do it while you feel some passion, some excitement, some enthusiasm.

Don't think, deliberate or plan. Jump in.

Go with your "gut" feeling and trust your intuition.

Follow up one action with another and then another and then another…and soon it will become second nature as the momentum carries you along and you feel comfortable in your new modus operandi.

ACTION TIPS - SECRET #2

1. Now that you have decided to be rich (or whatever else you want), think of one thing you can do to achieve that goal...and then do it. Take one action on it. See how good it makes you feel. How empowering it is.

2. Now take another action and another. Each day, do at least one thing that moves you closer to what you want and experience how energizing that is...and how each action, no matter how small, motivates you to take another and another and another. Then, just keep that momentum going with small, incremental (sometimes lateral) actions, the purpose of which is to just keep you in motion. You will notice that no matter how small your steps, they will multiply exponentially and often mushroom into huge, wonderful consequences and opportunities.

3. Get a copy of Mark Burnett's book, *Jump In...Even If You Don't Know How to Swim* and read it. It's a fast, easy read that you can even skim. It's more the energy of the book that I'm interested in you experiencing than any particular information, although reading how he accomplished what he did will certainly inspire and motivate you and get you to realize that you can do anything you want...and you can begin to do it now – right where you are.

4. Honestly assess where you are now – what your strengths, talents, interests, assets are now – and begin from there. Don't try to "reinvent the wheel." Start with what you have, know and are good at and are perhaps, even doing to some degree already and use that as your launching point.

   Once you begin making money, you can always expand or change what you are doing if you want. For now, just get started in the easiest, simplest, most expeditious way possible. Focus in on what you want to develop and can do easily and quickly to begin generating immediate income. You can always build on it later.

5. Do something fun...Go dancing, see a zany comedy, get together with a friend and laugh. Don't think or talk about any of this.

6. Go someplace wealthy people normally go or do something affluent people do. Put yourself in their circle and mingle with them. Go with the feeling that you belong there and put yourself in the place and position to meet some – even one – rich, influential person. Even if you don't meet anyone this first time, you will feel differently about yourself just being there and doing that.

   Some suggestions – Visit Cartier or some high-priced

clothing or jewelry store and let the store personnel wait on you as a potential customer, browse a model home in a very upscale new development and ask questions, get brochures, inquire about cost and amenities, always thinking of yourself and feeling like you are there to one day buy if you choose to. Lose yourself in the experience. Be there totally. Be fully present and always with the belief that you deserve to be there and belong.

7. Practice hearing and listening to your body when it tells you something feels right or does not feel right. Start with something small at first like deciding which street to turn down to find a parking space; or the next time you go shopping, notice if you are making a frivolous purchase, how it feels in your body…if it feels like you should make the purchase or not. Once you learn to hear, listen to and trust what I call your "body language," you can begin to develop that dialogue, rapport and trust with larger, more important things.

8. And finally, determine your own 80/20 factor. Figure out what you are spending 80% of your time on that is giving you only a 20% return. Most of the time, it is just a matter of no longer busying yourself with endless errands and allowing yourself and your time to be consumed by trivial, unimportant things that keep you busy, but sap your energy and get you nowhere.

It is also a matter of taking the time to think about the 80/20 factor and focusing on what you need to do that will give you the most immediate and largest return for the least amount of effort and time. THAT is working smarter, rather than harder. All the people of great accomplishment do that – they work smart, not necessarily hard. Which doesn't mean they don't work hard, but when you are working smart, when you are going with your energy flow, the work seems like play and is so much easie…It just flows and you accomplish more with effortless ease.

AND REMEMBER TO ENJOY . . . PROSPER . . . AND DARE TO BE RICH!

"High achievement always takes place in the framework of high expectation."

Charles F. Kettering

Secret #3

Believe

The ancient Roman poet Virgil said, "They can because they think they can." Or to phrase it more accurately...They can because they *believe* they can. But even that does not say it all because the words "think" and "believe" have come to be so limited and limiting in our modern culture.

We have overused these phrases so, that they have become largely one-dimensional phrases (at best – 1 ½ dimensional, when you add some feeling to belief) that get stuck in our minds and rarely go beyond our mental processes which by themselves, rarely accomplish what we desire, and often even, confuse, hamper and interfere with our getting what we desire.

The impetus and the fuel for achieving our desires come from something other than our mind. Our mind is often cluttered, unfocused, overwhelmed and has to be controlled by something more powerful, more focused, more unstoppable than the mind – and that is our will...or our spirit...or that 'thing" inside us that drives us; what Dylan Thomas calls "thru the green fuse drives the flower."

It's that "thing," that "force" inside us – that mental process infused with faith, passion and expectation – that makes all things possible and real to us even when everything appears to indicate the opposite.

A STORY

Again, I am reminded of the story of Christopher Columbus – a story I never thought much about my entire life. I just remember learning in grade school that Columbus discovered America, and that was the end of it.

But now, as an adult with a deep awareness and appreciation of the miracles we can achieve with our will and our power of belief, I am awed by the story of Christopher Columbus which was brought to life for me so clearly by what Andy Andrews wrote in his book *The Traveler's*

Gift, in which a modern man named David, travels though time and lands on Columbus's ship with him.

Columbus tells David that he was humiliated for years because of his belief that the world was round and that he could establish a new trade route to the east by sailing west.

But even this sustained public scorn could not dissuade Columbus from his firm, unwavering conviction to pursue his dream. No, not his dream...his unequivocal knowing that the earth was round, not flat...and that he could sail around it, without falling off.

Even the fact the he was the only one who believed this at the time and that everyone thought he was crazy, did not dampen his fervor and enthusiasm – his surety in what he believed.

And his belief fostered such an unshakable expectation of success in him, that even after he and his men had been sailing for 69 days seeing nothing but water and ocean, he was still able to categorically tell them and David that tomorrow, on the 70th day when the sun rose, they would see land straight ahead of them.

And because of this unwavering belief in his dream, because of his unshakable expectation, he knew that all obstacles to the accomplishment of it would be obliterated and its success assured. He knew that this kind of belief makes you "unstoppable."

Do you realize how incredible that is – to believe that at that time? What faith and courage it took for

Columbus to persist for almost 20 years until he got his funding, got his armada and crew together, and embarked on his exhilarating journey into the unknown...into uncharted waters to discover a new world!

His passion fueled his belief, and his belief buttressed his passion – a belief in something no one else believed...a belief in something neither he nor anyone else could see or prove...a belief in something so fantastic and intangible, and yet so utterly real for him.

That is the kind of belief I am talking about when I say "belief" is the third step in becoming rich or getting anything you want. I am talking about belief as faith... belief as trust...belief that is rooted in passion and such conviction that it becomes a knowing. I am talking about a belief that inhabits you so completely, that the reality of it, the accomplishment of it, the "living" of it is never in question.

This kind of belief radiates out from the believer and acts as a magnetic field as well as a laser. So not only does it magnetize to you everything and everyone you need to achieve your desired goal, it also keeps you focused, so that it is often not even necessary to consciously make an effort and mentally think of the "how" as you move inexorably toward what you want.

Yes – *inexorably* – what a fabulous word! It captures the essence of that process this kind of belief initiates and sustains. Webster defines *inexorable* as "not to be stopped by entreaty of any kind; relentless."

FULL-BODIED BELIEF

So when you have this kind of "full-bodied" belief, you cannot be dissuaded, stymied or seduced by any form of entreaty – not by doubts, questions, not even pleading. You literally become unstoppable and you will reach your desired goal...guaranteed!

This kind of belief is literally like jet propulsion fuel – it propels you directly to your goal. This kind of belief has you doing, not trying. This kind of belief has you always moving forward, not looking backward. In fact, you don't have time or any inclination to ever look back, to hesitate or to doubt...all of which literally become unthinkable in the respect that they are so alien, so foreign, that they never even enter your mind.

So, I am not talking about "positive thinking." I am referring instead, to something much more powerful, much more pervasive. I'm talking about expectation. It is not just a mental attitude that you have in your mind; it is a belief that you "embody." It lives and breathes in every cell of your body, so of course, it becomes real.

Of course, the belief becomes the reality because the expectation of success – an expectation infused with your passion, desire, unwavering faith, and trust...with an unshakable certainty – creates it.

This kind of certainty arises only when we are willing to get "out of our minds." I know that phrase sounds scary. When I was growing up, "out of your mind" meant that you were crazy.

But I begin to wonder more and more if when the phrase originated, it meant something totally different. If perhaps it didn't refer to someone who was willing to go beyond the boundaries of the rational mind that analyzes and reacts to things based on what it perceives with our five senses. If perhaps it didn't refer to those individuals who were visionaries in the truest sense of the word – people who saw beyond what is obvious.

VISIONING

And that is why knowing and believing work where visualizations and affirmations often do not. Visualizations and affirmations are often mouthed and usually, thought about a great deal. But I have found that so often, when a person says an affirmation or consciously does visualizations, they do both kind of one-dimensionally – lacking any real passion; strong, full-bodied belief, so they are therefore, not pervasive.

I find affirmations are frequently little more than lip-service. Plus, the mere act of affirming puts the very thing you are affirming into question, making you even more aware of the fact that you are affirming it just because you do not have it; and you therefore become even more aware of what it is you feel you are lacking. This is very insidious because it all takes place on a very subtle, subliminal level – a level which is very powerful.

So an affirmation often serves to remind a person of the very thing that he or she feels the lack of and is therefore affirming. In so doing, it often undermines the very belief that the affirmation is trying to affirm.

The same is true of visualizations. If they are not done with an intense, passionate, unwavering belief buttressing them, they become mere reminders of what you *don't* have that you want...and actually hinder you in getting what you want.

What I call visioning – which is not a consciously initiated activity – is what I find really works. And the beauty of visioning is that it is not anything you have to do. It just happens.

Once you have a burning desire to be rich (or anything else you want) and decide to do, be or have it, and then act on your decision; once you proceed to act with a strong, passionate, unwavering, full-bodied pervasive belief that you will get it...the visioning just appears and grows larger and more real, fleshing out and becoming more substantial every day and with every act you take.

You begin to live what it is that you desire as what you desire becomes so real, so palpable for you that it is no longer just a thought, a need or a desire. It is something that you find yourself living and breathing every single day. So it takes on a life and momentum of its own and carries you along.

It is almost as though the result or the end you are

visioning becomes your starting point. The end becomes the beginning because what you want is so real for you that you are already experiencing it as a reality and your daily life is then, just moving you through the actions and activities that are catching your life up with the reality you are already experiencing, living and already know and feel with certainty is real.

If you have any doubts about this or feel at all confused about how it works, remember Christopher Columbus describing to David, the new world that wasn't even visible to the eye yet! This is what I call *full-bodied visioning*...being a *visionary*...living "as if".

A lot of people say, "Oh, you mean 'Fake it 'till you make it,'"...and I say, "No, I don't!" This has nothing to do with faking anything. This has to do with believing something so much that you see it "in the flesh," "in the world...in your world" already. This has to do with certainty, with living with such a certainty, that the certainty creates the reality.

It's a conundrum almost like the perennial "chicken and the egg." Which comes first? Does the reality you are visioning, living and feeling already exist in some ideal form, as Plato tells us it does...and are you just seeing into that ideal reality before it becomes manifest? Or are your belief and passion so strong that they are creating the reality?

Perhaps the best explanation is that your strong, unwavering belief acts like the *organizing principle* –

creating order out of chaos, creating the reality you want and envision out of a myriad of possible realities – like the kaleidoscope creates a unique reality each time you turn it, out of the disparate, unorganized elements and possibilities.

Without getting deeply into quantum physics and philosophy, what I am saying is that your thoughts – your beliefs – when they are infused with passion, constancy and intensity are as powerful as a laser and a magnet. They can create order out of chaos; they can create something where there seemingly was nothing before, and your beliefs can create and bring to you whatever it is you desire. They can make you rich, happy, healthy, succesful – anything you want. You just have to believe.

Claude Bristol tells us, in his wonderful book, *The Magic of Believing*, that with belief, we can manifest whatever we want because belief exerts a "strange power" that causes miracles to happen – things for which we have no explanation.

Oh, he's not talking about your ordinary beliefs, but about belief that is deep-rooted – "a firm and positive conviction that goes through every fiber of your being"… what I call *full-bodied belief.*

This kind of belief is what sets the law of attraction into action and activates serendipity…bringing you and what you desire together. And since everything is energy, this serendipitous law of attraction in action is so strong, that it elevates your energy level and creates a new energy frequency that acts like a huge magnet, bringing you and what you desire together and helping to make your dreams come true.

So if you really want something – whether it's to be rich, famous, happy, healthy, to meet your soul-mate, write a book...whatever it is you want – just decide to be it, have it, do it; then *do* something to achieve it and keep on doing things. And as you do, begin to live it – allow yourself to live it – to believe with every fibre of your being that you *deserve* to do, be and have it; that you *can* do, be and have it...and that you *will* do, be and have it.

Expect it and live as though what you expect is on its way to you. You have to believe in miracles; otherwise they won't happen. When you believe in them and expect them, you create the space for them and invite them into your life like a welcomed guest.

Napoleon Hill said, "Faith [belief] is the starting point of all accumulation of riches." Start now to accumulate and claim the riches that are yours.

BELIEVE!

BELIEVE THAT YOU <u>DESERVE</u> TO BE RICH . . .

BELIEVE THAT YOU <u>CAN</u> BE RICH . . .

BELIEVE THAT YOU <u>WILL</u> BE RICH . . .

<u>EXPECT</u> TO BE RICH . . .

AND THEN JUST <u>LET IT HAPPEN!</u>

ACTION TIPS - SECRET #3

First – let me reiterate that it **is not necessary to do any of these suggestions or exercises**. Just read each chapter in one sitting, with your full attention – no multi-tasking, no interruptions, no distractions. Each chapter is enough to help you accomplish what you want.

Also, when you read the chapters, do not underline or highlight anything as you read. Doing so just interferes with the momentum and stops the smooth, osmotic flow of energy from the chapter through to you. Underlining and highlighting alter the entire process and the connection between you and the material you are reading by putting the receptive, responsive side of you (your right brain) in direct conflict with the "take charge" side (your left brain).

I offer these suggestions, exercises and homework with each step only for those who feel they want to do more.

1. Focus in specifically on what you want and then let yourself embody it and inhabit it completely. What you want should be specific and concrete – not just "I want to be rich" or "I want to be happy." You need to determine and focus in on what you want to do with the money; what will make you happy. Focus in on these and then just begin living and acting as though you already have or are it. Don't complicate the process

with visualizations or affirmations. Don't mentalize (my own word that I just invented) it. Just do it...Let yourself go – trust, believe, have faith and let the result be your starting point and begin living from there. It works! It really does.

2. Read *The Magic of Believing* by Claude Bristol. It's a fabulous book published in the 1940's that is simple, direct and gets right to the heart of things.

3. Begin noticing the small miracles and "little serendipities" that occur in your life – often every day, but most people never notice them. When you open up and awaken to something, it begins to happen more and more.

THE DARE . . .

So, I dare you to . . .

      Dare to Be Happy

      Dare to Dream

      Dare to Prosper

Dare to feel the Rapture of Being Alive

  Dare to Be All That You Can Be

    Dare to Be Rich!

"... I believe in Bach's Law which says, 'If anything can go right, it must!'"

Marcus Bach
The World of Serendipity

5

Secret #4

SERENDIPITY

Now that you've decided to be rich, have acted on that decision and expect to be successful – how do you guarantee that the synergy between these first three steps will work?

What's that secret ingredient – that magical fourth step – the key to unlocking the continuous flow of wealth, riches, happiness and success...with effortless ease? Serendipity...

What is serendipity? Serendipity means that you stop second-guessing yourself. It means eliminating your *hidden shoulds*.

SILENCING THE HIDDEN SHOULDS

What are the *hidden shoulds*? They are those silent, subliminal voices in your head that are so insidious, they prevent you from being happy, rich, successful…or whatever you want. It's those *hidden shoulds* whispering in your ear, telling you that you *should* be scared, you *should* be anxious, you *should* worry, you *should* be upset…you *should* this…you *should* that…until you don't even know what you are feeling anymore, because these *shoulds* have gotten you so out of touch with your genuine feelings.

It's almost as though we are actors playing a role the way we think it *should* be played, rather than how we want to play it, how we see it being played, how we feel it needs to be played (which we don't even know anymore because we are so focused on and conditioned to how we think it should be played). So, we don't dare deviate from those hidden stage directions that those *hidden shoulds* are giving us. We don't even allow ourselves the luxury of getting in touch with what we genuinely feel. But it is these genuine feelings, that will catapult you into authentic living…and the riches you desire.

That is the engine behind serendipity. Serendipity is not an accident and it's not an occurrence – as many people think. It's a force that is released when we liberate ourselves from our *hidden shoulds*. And when we do this, we are in the moment...and that's really what serendipity is all about – why it is so organic and alive and why it works – because we are in the moment all the time, so we can be responsive, present and alive and therefore, in touch with what we are feeling, so we can take action.

So how do you become serendipitously rich? It's simple, but not easy because you need to eliminate the one habit that is so tenacious, so subtle, so insidious that it stops most people from ever becoming rich...or whatever else they want.

THE WILLING SUSPENSION OF DISBELIEF

I remember reading years ago, that when you enter a movie theatre, you must enter it with "a willing suspension of disbelief." You must leave your logical, rational mind outside of the theatre. In fact, you must leave your mind completely out of it, so that you enter the world of the story – the world created by the writer, director and actors – totally, whole-heartedly, unconditionally.

So that you don't keep asking "how that" or "why this." You don't say, "Wait a minute, that doesn't make sense," because the rules are different in the world they have created and that you have entered...and in that world, everything *does* make sense. You just need to accept it and go with the flow.

It's the same in your life – you are the writer, director, and lead actor – and the world you create has its own rules where the impossible becomes possible, the impossible becomes probable, and anything…no…everything is possible.

This is the world of your dreams, which is not the same as a fantasy. A fantasy is imaginary; a dream is real. And it's not the same as a hope, a desire or a wish either. None of these has any foundation under them. There is little substance to them other than a moderate (even sometimes a strong) emotional one

But a dream is something that grows out of who you are, what you value…your deepest desires. A dream is something that the muses bring to us so we can realize it. Goethe, the 18th century German philosopher says, "Whatever you can do, or dream you can, begin it. Boldness has genius, power and magic in it."

So dreams have passion. Dreams have power. Dreams are the starting point of great things. And if you dream of being rich…you can be!

THE VOICE OF SHOULD

So, what is the one habit you must break – *that voice of should*. You need to shut it out…and turn it off. It's a voice that is so loud and so pervasive that most people don't even hear anything else; while at the same time, they don't even realize they are hearing this "voice of should".

This *"voice of should"* is the voice that gnaws away at your confidence, your trust, your faith, patience, and peace of mind. It keeps telling you that "you *should* be worried, you *should* be afraid"...when all the while, deep down inside, you know you are doing what you need to do, you are moving in the direction you want to, and that everything will be just fine.

But that voice says, "Yeah, but it's not now, so you *should* worry...you *should* be afraid."

But if you are willing to trust what you *know*, not what you see; if you are willing to trust your *gut* and not your mind; if you are willing to trust *yourself* and not what others say; if you are willing to hold firm to your dream... then you *will* be serendipitously rich. If you are willing to live richly – to be rich *while* you are becoming rich – then you are serendipitously rich.

I am not talking about positive thinking, not talking about visualizations or affirmations. I'm not talking about faking it till you make it. There is nothing fake about being serendipitously rich.

Being serendipitously rich has less to do with your mind and your heart than it does with your gut, less to do with what you feel and what you think than with what you know.

So, being serendipitously rich is actually not a step or a secret. It is rather when everything comes together, coalesces and becomes your life. This can happen while you are implementing the three secrets, or after, but since the three secrets are not linear, but rather associative and intertwined, becoming serendipitously rich is woven into the very fabric of each and all of these secrets. Like a hologram, the whole is contained in the parts.

THE FACTS AND BEING RICH

Being serendipitously rich is that moment when you no longer backslide into the habit of worrying about money and being afraid just because what you are experiencing at the moment – the facts – do not indicate that you are rich.

What are facts anyway? Most people believe that facts are like laws or mandates from some expert or higher authority; that facts are written in stone and cannot be changed; that facts are what they are…immutable and unchanging.

But facts are just a statement of what exists at that very moment. They're temporary and situational. They describe a present moment observable reality. But facts can change and reality can change. So, facts are not reality. Facts are not "the truth." *The world is flat* was a fact…until it became not a fact. *Matter and energy are different* was a fact…until it became not a fact.

BEING RICH *BEFORE* YOU ARE RICH

So, to be serendipitously rich, you have to be willing to be rich *before* you are actually rich. You have to be willing to see, experience, and live what you *know* to be true, despite what the facts tell you *seems* to be true.

You have to be willing to be who and what you know you are even though others may not be able to see it yet, even though you may not be able to tangibly prove it yet. You have to dare to believe, dare to allow yourself to know what you know – despite all outward appearances – and to act on what you know and to live it.

You have to be willing to give yourself *permission* to be rich even though you do not yet have the money to prove that you are…even though you may feel like you are being crazy, or hypocritical or lying or in denial or maybe just plain delusional, but somewhere, deep down of inside you…*because you have made the decision to be rich* and successful, you *know* that your being rich is no longer a matter of *if*, only *when*. And then it becomes a question only of, "Do I dare live like I am rich even though I don't have the money yet?"

And then suddenly, one day, there is no more backsliding…not even the thought of it, because it is now so inconceivable to you, so alien that you can't even imagine worrying about money or being scared or doubting… because being rich is now your life and the fact that you don't have the money yet doesn't even seem to matter. It becomes totally immaterial because you *know* (not just think or believe) that it is on its way…you *know* you are rich…and you begin to savor and enjoy being *delightfully, delectably, deliciously...serendipitously rich* – wholeheartedly, totally and unconditionally.

SERENDIPITOUSLY RICH...THE IMAGE BECOMES THE REALITY

Then one day, quite unceremoniously, the money comes. It gets deposited into your bank account and your account grows and grows...and serendipitously rich becomes factually rich while you have been too busy living your serendipitously rich life to even think about money, worry about money, be anxious about money or plan for money. You have been too busy living a serendipitously rich life to even notice that suddenly, serendipitously rich and factually rich have become one and the same...that the invisible facts – the riches that you have known, felt and claimed all along *once you decided to be rich* – are now visible for everyone to see.

And then, it no longer matters if everyone can see the money now because being serendipitously rich has enriched your life so, that the money – once all important while it was lacking – is suddenly only one small part of your wealth now that it is abundant and flowing...now that you are doing what you love...now that you are in control of your life and your finances...because now you know what you need to do, what you *can* do to get *anything* you want...even to get rich.

And being serendipitously rich creates a new reality – or rather, new facts – for everyone to see. So the facts change...and just like "the world is flat" and just like "matter and energy are two different things" were replaced by new facts...the facts of your life are replaced by new facts as you step into and claim this new reality...this reality that says, that proves, that shows everyone that... *YES...I **am** rich – I am factually, delightfully, delectably, deliciously...serendipitously rich for all to see*!

QUALITIES OF SERENDIPITY

In the Moment

Responsive

Your True Feelings

Facts are not what they seem...They can change

Permission

No Shoulds

Letting go

Reality is what you experience, not what you see

Openness

Wonder

Delight

Your Authentic Self

*Allows you to experience reality **before** it becomes a physical reality*

SHOULDS TO DELIGHT IN . . .

The *voice of should* is very powerful – so use it to your advantage and benefit.

Here is a new list of **shoulds** *for you to delight in…enjoy…savor…live by…and…even…to get rich by*!

Feel free to add to the list…and remember to always phrase your new *shoulds* in the affirmative, according to what you *do want*, not what you don't want. (If you focus on what you don't want, that is what sticks in your mind and where your attention automatically goes, since our brains seem to respond to the word [noun, verb, adjective, adverb] not the qualifier that comes before it.)

I *should* be happy

I *should* be delighted

I *should* be full of joy

I *should* be loved

I *should* have life easy

I *should* be successful

I *should* be healthy

I *should* have lots of money

I *should* be rich

I *should* have what I want

I *should* feel empowered

I *should* feel vibrantly alive

I *should* do what I love and love what I do

I *should* love my life

I *should* be Delightfully, Delectably, Deliciously Rich...

I *should* be a Serendipitous Millionaire!

ACTION TIPS - SECRET #4

1. Begin eliminating those *hidden shoulds* that determine your experiences and shape your life. Begin with one – the one you think might be the easiest to eliminate.

   For example...the next time someone does or says something that could be hurtful to you, and the voice that tells you "I *should* be insulted" rears its head, stop and ask yourself if you really *are*. Really get in touch with your feelings and wade through the layers of social conditioning telling you what you should and should not feel.

   Let yourself move through the whole process of..."He/She shouldn't have said that"..."He/She ignored my needs"..."He/she was really rude and insulting"..."I *should* be insulted."

   Then ask yourself, "Am I? What am I *really* feeling?" Most of the time, you will discover that you aren't really insulted at all...and that the whole thing really isn't that important...that you can easily shrug it off with "Oh, well,"...or "So what," once you move through and beyond what you think you *should* feel!"

   See and feel how liberating that is. Then, once you eliminate one *hidden should,* move on to another, then another, and another, moving on to the more difficult ones that have to do with money (ie: I *should* worry about money, I *should* have to struggle to make money…you get the picture…) and then eliminating them one by one, so you can become *serendipitously rich*!

The first time you do this exercise, you will actually find yourself feeling shocked and astonished that you really don't care as much as you thought…that you are *not really* insulted, you are *not really* worried about money…even perhaps, not insulted (or worried) at all. It's an amazing exercise…and extraordinarily liberating!!

2. Give yourself permission to be rich (or happy, or successful, or healthy…or anything else you want).

It seems that deep down, we are all still (and always will be) little kids needing and wanting permission – permission to be happy…permission to have life easy…permission to be loved…permission to do what we want…permission to be rich…permission not to struggle.

I know it sounds crazy, but it's true. It seems most people – rich/poor, young/old, professional/blue collar, male/female, successful/struggling – operate under a hidden cloud of what Shirley MacLaine calls "underservability."

We struggle to get what we want (because we believe we are *supposed* to struggle) and then when we get it, we don't feel we deserve it, can't accept it, don't trust it...so we sabotage it. Then we continue to struggle even when we don't need to because that's what we think we are supposed to do...what we *should* do. (Again, there's that insidious *"voice of should"*!)

So give yourself unadulterated (interesting word!!!), unconditional, absolute permission to be rich! One way you can do this is to elicit it from one of your friends, mentors, spiritual guides, or what I call "your council of advisors." These are the people you love and trust (they can be living or not) who have only your best interests at heart.

You don't even need to have them all in one place. You can phone them, visit them, meet with them... or...You can call them together anytime you want in your mind, while walking, out in nature, in your favorite place, meditating, whatever. I actually find it much more effective to get permission from each one individually, usually the permission that means the most from that particular individual, although sometimes I do call the whole council together.

3. Read my book *Living Serendipitously...keeping the wonder alive*.

   I can't tell you how many people – all kinds, ages, genders, professions and jobs – have told me how liberating and empowering this book was for them because it gave them permission.

   Why am I recommending my own book? I always recommend the book I think is the best for whatever I am speaking about...and in this case, I believe this is the best book. So, why not recommend it? I recommend others' books when I think they're the best.

4. Do the "Dance of Should"—a crazy, impromptu, totally off-the-wall dance or movements...whatever comes to you and whatever you truly feel like doing in the moment...with no censorship, no critic, no judge.

   Remember (how could you forget?) the memorable dance Elaine did on *Seinfeld*? Or the dance Kevin James did in the film *Hitch*, when he was trying desperately to woo the rich heiress whom he loved, but was unable to contain the secretly mischievous, out-of-control little kid inside him on the dance floor?

   Doing something like that is liberating, fun, and

physically expresses your total disregard for those *hidden shoulds* that are trying to dictate the movements of your life.

Doing something like that gets you totally out of your rational, logical mind that sees and accepts only what is appropriate or reasonable ...and opens you up to the infinite possibilities of wider horizons.

5. Remember the exercise we did at the beginning of the book – throwing the water out of your front door? Well, do it again; only this time, with every heave of the bucket, declare (silently or out loud, whichever works best for you) that you are hurling out another *hidden should* that has been holding you back from being serendipitously rich!

6. Begin to live what you are dreaming of. Don't think about it, question it, wonder if it's possible, be afraid you look foolish...just do it!

Whatever your dream is – *feel it here, now, real*...and begin to live and act just like you would if it were real because it *is* real. And if you do this, soon it *will* be tangibly real.

Create the immediacy that makes the experience palpable – step into it with your whole heart – and live it. Do it now!

"The riches you receive will be in exact proportion to the definiteness of your vision, the fixity of your purpose, the steadiness of your faith and the depth of your gratitude."

Wallace D. Wattles
The Science of Getting Rich

Dare to be Rich

*B*eing rich is easy; not being rich is hard. This book is the rich person's guide to easy success.

Yes – I know that sounds like an oxymoron. You don't usually hear those two words together – "easy success" – but that is only because of years, decades and probably centuries of social conditioning that has been passed down, almost by rote, without question.

But success *is* easy – it is we who make it difficult.

Success *is* simple – it is we who complicate it. Success *is* fun – it is we who make it drudgery.

So, if success is so easy, why aren't more of us rich and happy and successful? Because we put up roadblocks, detour signs, big stop signs; we build walls and carve out gorges and imagine mountains; we become hard, inflexible, scared; we shrink and become small and timid and try to make ourselves invisible while all the while there is this greatness, this largeness inside us clamoring to get out.

We think we are intimidated by life, by others, by circumstances; but we are not. It is we who intimidate ourselves because on some level we all know and feel our greatness, yet we shrink from stepping into it.

We devise all kinds of methods to avoid ourselves, our greatness and stepping into and claiming the riches, success and abundance that are ours – like procrastination, a whole host of socially and personally acceptable subterfuges, and the entire gamut of defense mechanisms that enable us to still feel OK while avoiding our success and prosperity.

But OK is not good enough…and is certainly not acceptable on a long-term basis. In fact, feeling just OK is worse than feeling really bad on a long-term basis. As least when you feel really bad, you know something is wrong and know you need to take some action.

Feeling OK however, lulls you into a false sense of security and comfort – a complacency that dulls your mind, your senses, your perceptions and abilities. Feeling

OK siphons off your motivation, your passion, your zest for life, your curiosity, your sense of wonder, your desire to achieve, accomplish and aspire…slowly draining your energy and depleting your resources – very subtly and therefore, insidiously.

TAPPING INTO ABUNDANCE

Perhaps one of the reasons more people aren't rich and don't live abundantly is because they think abundance is something they have to create. Abundance is not something you create; it is something you tap into. And therefore, money is really something that is somehow "out there," just waiting for you to claim it.

Claude Bristol, in his book *The Magic of Believing*, tells the story of a friend of his who in the 1940's was building a boat, but needed an electric drill to complete it. He didn't want to buy one because he only needed it for a few months for this one particular project, and he couldn't rent it because then he had to return it every morning.

"Then he told me, [Bristol relates] 'I got thinking one night that somewhere there was a drill for me and I would have it placed in my hands.' The more I thought about it, the more I thought it possible."

Well – a few days later, he did get his drill. A friend found out he needed one and loaned it to him.

The key here however, is that Bristol's friend

realized that there was a drill for him "out there" and somehow it would find its way into his hands…and it did.

The same thing has happened to me over and over with money, things, people, etc. Last year, my son was visiting me in North Carolina and we were playing Horseshoes at the Inn nearby, but were missing one horseshoe. We looked and looked all over, but couldn't find the missing horseshoe.

So we played without it, sharing one of the horseshoes. And then – the strangest thing happened. I *knew* the missing horseshoe was there! I *felt* it. I can't explain how or why. So I stopped all activity, got quiet for a moment – and then walked right over to where the missing horseshoe was and lifted it up out of the bushes.

I have often had experiences like that, but this was different. This time I actually felt its presence – I *felt* the density or the vibration of the horseshoe…I *felt* its presence.

And perhaps, that's how it works with money too. Perhaps we just need to accept the fact that the money – the million dollars, the riches (or whatever else you want – your soul-mate, the perfect job, ideal house, etc.) are "out there" just waiting to be placed in your hands, in your life, in your bank account…waiting for you to find and claim them.

And perhaps, all we need to do is to get quiet and still – so we can feel the vibratory presence of the money, the person, the home we want and we will be led to it easily, naturally and effortlessly.

That actually happened to me when I was with my son again – in Freeport on Grand Bahama Island. We were in the casino – he was playing the tables and I was playing the quarter slot machines.

All of a sudden, I was literally directed – by some voice or "vibratory shift" perhaps – to leave the machine I was playing and go to a large, flashy, modern, automated dollar machine – a machine I never would have chosen to play.

As soon as I began playing that machine, I knew the winnings were there waiting for me to claim them. Every time I put my dollars in, I knew, I could feel some density, some vibration that told me…yes, it was getting closer and closer.

After playing the machine eight or ten times (I don't remember which) I won $1,000.00…and I wasn't the slightest bit surprised because I felt the money before it even got into my hands. I knew it was on its way to me – it was there waiting for me to claim it.

If I had not listened to the still small voice urging me to not only switch machines, but directing me to that specific machine…If I had not been responsive and decisive and not acted immediately as the voice was urging me to – *do it, do it now, now…now* – and if I had not believed unwaveringly in the outcome – everything would have been different.

So, each one of us is a co-creator in the affluence

we experience, the "riches" we enjoy with our attentiveness, our responsiveness, our decisiveness, our visioning and our belief.

BEGINNING WHERE YOU ARE

Being, becoming, getting rich…acquiring wealth and being affluent all begin with how you are in the world. If you move through life with generosity and graciousness… with l*argesse – a generosity of spirit or attitude* – then the leap to your finances is not so great; you are already tapped into abundance and just have to expand it to the world of your finances.

And I don't want it to sound overly metaphysical either. It's actually very practical, simple and ordinary – if you want to be rich, you cannot compartmentalize your life, your self and your spirit. You cannot live linearly, with a tight hold on your compliments, your graciousness, your generosity of spirit and then hope, pray, wish or expect that your finances will be overflowing and abundant. You need to overflow in all of life.

I remember taking a course in Hemingway in graduate school and learning that all of his heroes had a dual persona – a business self and a personal self. I thought that sounded absurd at the time…so artificial; until years later when I realized that many people actually do live their lives that way. Perhaps they are manipulative at work and then expect to be able to turn it off and be affectionate, compassionate and empathetic at home. Or perhaps they are goal oriented and driven at work and then expect to be able to be associative and *relate-able* (that is definitely not a word!) at home.

Often, they are tight and ungiving or ungracious in their relationships and daily living and then expect the riches to flow to them. It doesn't work that way. What we do...who we are every day...is what we will experience in our lives. If you want an unimpeded flow of money (friends, love, joy, success) you have to enter the flow... you have to participate in the unimpeded flow...you have to become a part of it.

You have to be willing to *live* richly to be, become and get rich. Money is not attracted to those who don't... and money finds those who do, an irresistible magnet. If you practice the very simple steps in this manual, you will become a magnet for all the riches you desire...and you will do it simply, easily, naturally and have fun doing it.

Enjoy . . . Prosper . . . and Dare to Be a Serendipitous Millionaire!

THE 4 SECRETS TO GETTING RICH

- **DECIDE** – *Intend, Commit, Make a Declaration*

- **ACT** – *Be an Active Dreamer, Ignite Your Passion, Just Do it, No Details*

- **BELIEVE** – *Trust, Go by Your Gut Feelings, Expect to Get What You Want*

- **SERENDIPITY** – *Eliminate the Hidden Shoulds, Dare to Be Rich **Before** You Are Rich*

• • • • • • • •

Any time you find yourself asking "Why Me?" change that to "Why not me?" It's got to be someone, so why not you?

ACTION TIPS FOR GETTING RICH

DECIDE – Commit. Your subconscious and those around you who can help you get what you desire, are not going to commit if you're not. Also, you need to decide so your subconscious knows what you want…almost as if you are letting it know what the assignment is. Like in *Mission Impossible* (the old TV series) – they were instructed to read their mission, commit it to memory and then destroy it…so it was indelibly imprinted on their psyche, physiology…their entire being.

ACT – Create momentum. Stir up the energy. Create a new force of inertia. Give direction, movement, energy.

BELIEVE – Anchors and fuels. Gives your dream both roots and wings. Lets you soar at the same time it lays foundation.

SERENDIPITY – Keeps you in the moment, so you can be responsive, present and alive…and therefore, in touch with what you are feeling…so you can take action…so you can be rich before you are actually rich.

Serendipity . . . is a faculty in you that expects, experiences and attracts the best.

Serendipity . . . is a faculty in you that enables you to experience the reality of a thing *before* it is even in the physical world . . . so your full-bodied ex-perience helps materialize it.

Serendipity . . . enables you to begin with the result – that which you desire.

Serendipity . . . makes your dream – your deepest desire – what you decide to do, be or have . . . *a fait accompli!*

THE DOUBLE DARE . . .

So, I double dare you to...

    Dare to Be Carefree

    Dare to Be Free-Spirited

    Dare to Trust What You Know

    Dare to Be Rich Before You Are Rich

    Dare to Be a
Serendipitous Millionaire!

About the Author

Madeleine Kay is the Best Selling Author of *Serendipitously Rich* and *Living Serendipitously*. One of the most popular and unique success and prosperity coaches in the country, she is considered America's leading expert on *serendipity*.

Profiled in both *Who's Who of American Women* and *Who's Who in the World*, "Madeleine Kay is an expert at helping people live the life they usually only dream of," says Napoleon Hill Foundation CEO, Don Green.

A successful advertising executive, who was President and Creative Director of her own advertising/marketing/public relations agency, Kay is also a former Writing Instructor at the University of Miami and Tel Aviv University, wrote commentaries for the CBS affiliate in Miami, was an international fashion and photographic model, and an internationally acclaimed writer and success coach.

Now she brings the wisdom, passion and playfulness of serendipity sprinkled with her own unique brand of practical, down-to-earth common sense to the world of money and finance to help people get, claim and enjoy the riches they desire.

Books by Madeleine Kay

Serendipitously Rich...
How to Get Delightfully, Delectably, Deliciously Rich (or anything else you want) in 7 <u>Ridiculously</u> Easy Steps

Changing *if* I am rich to *when* I am rich has never been simpler...or more fun. Refreshingly original and excitingly new, *Serendipitously Rich* will not only motivate and inspire you – it will activate your "on" switch, your "go" switch, your whatever it is that makes you "do" something switch, so you can stop struggling and start getting rich (and everything else you want)...with effortless ease and unmitigated joy.

Living Serendipitously...keeping the wonder alive

A lively and joyful read, *Living Serendipitously* gets you to be an *active dreamer*, who is living your dreams, not just thinking about them. It captures the joyful essence of "the art of living" and shows you how to feel deliciously *alive*, vibrant and happy every day of your life...no matter what your circumstances. Einstein said, "There are only two ways to live your life – as though nothing is a miracle or as though *everything* is a miracle." *Living Serendipitously* aligns us with the *everything*.

Living with Outrageous Joy

Joy is contagious…joy is revitalizing…joy is what every one of us wants to feel more of in our lives. This charming little gift book will re-ignite that feeling of joy in your life and your passion for living. Playfully inspiring and motivating, *Living with Outrageous Joy* will delight and revitalize you. It will open you up to the joy and adventure of living your life to the fullest every single day… unleashing in you that feeling of aliveness that so many of us are longing to feel.

The 7 Secrets to Living with Joy and Riches

Joy and riches…isn't that what everyone wants? This charming gift book will delight and inspire you…and help you bring more of both into your life. You will find yourself picking it up over and over again, throughout the day, to savor the deliciously compelling exuberance and wisdom you will find on every page. A fabulous gift for everyone you know…and an indispensable personal companion.

The UMM Factor…(what you need in order to succeed)

This groundbreaking book about passion, purpose and prosperity shows us the three things everyone must have in order to succeed. Without all three, it is possible to succeed, but not likely. With them – your success is guaranteed. What are these three magical things? She calls them *The UMM Factor.*

SCATS...*scattered thoughts on just about everything*

Madeleine Kay's version of scatting is writing that is spontaneous, responsive and alive. It's fun, it's visceral... and delightfully original. Scatting is a musical term for a type of jazz singing that uses improvised vocal sounds, instead of words, to create unique and original musical melodies. Associated mostly with Ella Fitzgerald – one of the greatest scat singers in jazz history...and the music of the swing and big band era – scatting offers pure creative joy and freedom, and that's exactly what Kay's scats capture. This unique collection of scattered thoughts on just about everything will inspire, motivate, amuse, touch and delight you...and might even get you scatting too!

Savoring Life...Not Just Working at It
8 Principles for Living a Delicious Life

Life is meant to be savored, not just worked at. The dictionary defines savor as a verb meaning to delight in, to enjoy. Yet the more we learn, the more we seem to do – to make ourselves better or our lives richer. Most people work so hard at self-improvement, that their lives are anything but fun, full of joy...or delight. Their life becomes, in fact, like a huge assignment constantly looming over them. To experience life however, to live it – you must be engaged with life...you must savor it. Madeleine Kay's recipe for savoring life is simple. Her 8 principles for living a delicious life are things every one of us can do...and probably will, now that Kay has pointed them out to us in such a "delicious" way!

Internet Success for Beginners...7 Secrets Revealed

A true guide for real beginners, techno-phobes and techno-dummies, who want to begin an internet business...but haven't got a clue where or how to begin. This book introduces you to some very basic internet business possibilities...and walks you through exactly what you need to do to set them up, showing you the simplest, easiest, and most inexpensive (in some cases, even free) ways to do this. It even gives you websites, phone numbers and contact information for all the online resources you will need to do this.

Internet Success for Beginning Entrepreneurs...
7 Secrets Revealed

An excellent guide for novice and expanding entrepreneurs. Whether you are a techno-phobe or techno-dummy who wants to start an internet business, but haven't got a clue where or how to begin...or you are actually computer savvy and are just looking for new, innovative ways to create an internet business…this book introduces you to some very exciting and do-able internet business possibilities and walks you through exactly what you need to do to set them up, showing you the simplest, easiest, and most inexpensive (in some cases, even free) ways to do this. It even gives you websites, phone numbers and contact information for all the online resources you will need to get you started now, setting up your own successful internet business.

Internet Success…12 Secrets Revealed

Focused on what is simple, fast, easy and inexpensive, this book will help you start your own internet business with little or no technical knowledge or know-how and with little or no money. It tells you – as simply and succinctly as possible – twelve really simple, easy-to-do, inexpensive secrets about creating success online, so you not only don't have to spend years learning it all…but you actually have fun doing it. (It combines Kay's first two books in her internet marketing series – *Internet Success for Beginners* and *Internet Success for Beginning Entrepreneurs* – in one volume.)

The Serendipity Handbook

This personal handbook tells you everything you ever wanted to know about serendipity! Both elusive and compelling to most of us, serendipity is often defined as "a happy accident." But it's not an accident at all, Madeleine Kay tells us. "Serendipity is a faculty within us that finds, elicits and responds to the best in life and all it has to offer," she says. "It's that quality in us that creates order out of chaos, possibility out of potential...and reality out of possibility – the organizing principle that designs, directs and creates the life we want."

Coming Soon

How Will I Ever Get Over My Happy Childhood (Stories)

This collection of first person stories is original, refreshing and deliciously compelling with its zany characters and stories that will touch and delight you...and that you will long remember. These stories will make you laugh, make you cry, make you feel the sheer joy of being a human being as you realize how crazy and wonderful...how absurdly, and sometimes hilariously imperfect we are. Exquisitely written, they will take you through the whole gamut of emotions and quite literally, "knock your socks off" – so grab onto your hats and enjoy the ride!

. . . .

Madeleine Kay is the Founder of the Serendipity Day Holiday, celebrated August 18th . You can learn about this exciting new event and how to live serendipitously all year long at…www.serendipitydayholiday.com

Receive a FREE copy of *The Serendipity Handbook* at…www.facebook.com/serendipityday

Also receive a FREE *7 Myths About Money* E-course and E-book at…www.madeleinekay.com

. . . .

Follow Madeleine's blog online at...
www.madeleinekaylive.com

For personal one-on-one coaching or consulting, contact Madeleine at...www.madeleinekay.com

Check out Madeleine's collection of personal and pocket sized journals at...www.amazon.com

NOTES

NOTES

NOTES

www.ingramcontent.com/pod-product-compliance
Lightning Source LLC
Chambersburg PA
CBHW030755180526
45163CB00003B/1035